# Poetry from Texas College Students

Li Qingzhao, 1084-1155

# Poetry from Texas College Students

Edited by
## Gretchen Johnson

LITERARY PRESS
**LAMAR UNIVERSITY**

ISBN: 978-1-942956-28-0
Library of Congress Control Number:  2016942709

Portraits of famous poets: each wrote when
about the age of the writers in this anthology.
  Li Qingzhao, 1084-1155
  Elizabeth Barrett Browning, 1806-1861
  Emily Dickinson, 1830-1836
  William Butler Yeats, 1865-1939
  Manuel Ortiz Guerrero, 1897-1933

Lamar University Literary Press
Beaumont, Texas

Dedicated to emerging poets in Texas and beyond

Elizabeth Barrett Browning, 1806-1861

# Acknowledgments

Without the cooperation of the English professors across Texas, I would not have received the mass of submissions I was sent in order to see this project through. Thank you to each teacher who sent your students my way and helped them see their ambitions of publication realized.

And thank you to all the students who submitted your work. This book is for you.

Poetry from Lamar University Literary Press

Charles Behlen, *Failing Heaven*
Alan Berecka, *With Our Baggage*
David Bowles, *Flower, Song, Dance: Aztec and Mayan Poetry*
Jerry Bradley, *Crownfeathers and Effigies*
Matthew Brennan, *One Life*
Paul Christensen, *The Jack of Diamonds is a Hard Card to Play*
Chip Dameron, *Waiting for an Etcher*
William Virgil Davis, *The Bones Poems*
Jeffrey DeLotto, *Voices Writ in Sand*
Mimi Ferebee, *Wildfires and Atmospheric Memories*
Larry Griffin, *Cedar Plums*
Ken Hada, *Margaritas and Redfish*
Michelle Hartman, *Disenchanted and Disgruntled*
Michelle Hartman, *Irony and Irreverence*
Katherine Hoerth, *Goddess Wears Cowboy Boots*
Lynn Hoggard, *Motherland*
Gretchen Johnson, *A Trip Through Downer, Minnesota*
Ulf Kirchdorfer, *Chewing Green Leaves*
Janet McCann, *The Crone at the Casino*
Erin Murphy, *Ancilla*
Laurence Musgrove, *Local Bird*
Dave Oliphant, *The Pilgrimage, Selected Poems: 1962-2012*
Kornelijus Platelis, *Solitary Architectures*
Carol Coffee Reposa, *Underground Musicians*
Jan Seale, *The Parkinson Poems*
Carol Smallwood, *Water, Earth, Air, Fire, and Picket Fences*
Glen Sorestad, *Hazards of Eden*
W.K. Stratton, *Ranchero Ford/ Dying in Red Dirt Country*
Wally Swist, *Invocation*
Jonas Zdanys (ed.), *Pushing the Envelope, Epistolary Poems*

For information on these and other Lamar Literary Press books go to
www.Lamar.edu/literarypress

# Foreword

This book is a celebration—a celebration of the poetic minds of college students across the state of Texas, a celebration of the power that putting a particular string of words together in a carefully crafted form can create, a celebration of the joy a reader feels in discovering the untapped talent of an emerging writer, and a celebration of the thrill that writer feels in seeing his/her poetry printed in a published book.

When I was first presented with the opportunity to edit this collection, I knew I couldn't pass it up. As a poet and teacher of creative writing, the idea of giving students a chance to submit their work to a professionally printed anthology excited me. Even now, ten years into my teaching career, I can still easily recall the feeling of being a student writer starving to be heard. This book gives students that platform, and, as you will see, they are worth listening to.

I once heard a fellow writer say that a good book of poems needs to have at least one poem that speaks to each reader in some way because every reader will experience a different emotional response from the act of reading a book. As an editor, I kept this idea in mind while selecting the poems to be included. Poems were not selected to display my own biases, in terms of subject matter or form. Instead I tried to include poems from writers of various backgrounds, writing about a diversity of subjects, and poems that employ differing methods of delivery. It was important that the book didn't become a display of merely my own preferences but that any reader could pick up the book and mine for his/her own poetic gems. The one common trait of all the poems selected is that they each showcase an understanding of the poetic form and succeed in using language to stir up an emotional response from a reader.

To read a poem is to take a trip to that place where a person's intellect and passions intersect. To stand in that place can sometimes feel as endless as a sunrise on the plains of the Texas Panhandle, so take a seat, and travel through the minds of college students across Texas to see where their words will lead you. You won't be disappointed.

Gretchen Johnson

Emily Dickinson, 1830-1836

# CONTENTS

Winners of the Lamar University Literary Literary Press student writing contest for best poem:

First Place
   "Chronicles of a Forlorn Woman" by Onyx Bei
Second Place
   "Saw a Wild Thing" by Trampas Smith
Third Place

   "When I Was Jesus" by Bryan Owens

We . . . talked of poetry.
I said, 'A line will take us hours maybe;
Yet if it does not seem a moment's thought,
Our stitching and unstitching has been naught.
Better go down upon your marrow-bones
And scrub a kitchen pavement, or break stones
Like an old pauper, in all kinds of weather;
For to articulate sweet sounds together
Is to work harder than all these, and yet
Be thought an idler by the noisy set
Of bankers, schoolmasters, and clergymen
The martyrs call the world.'
   —William Butler Yeats, "Adam's Curse"


Poetry is simply the most beautiful, impressive, and widely
effective mode of saying things, and hence its importance.
   —Matthew Arnold


Writing a poem is discovering.
   —Robert Frost


Great poetry is always written by somebody straining to go
beyond what he can do.
   —Stephen Spender


write poetry, for God's sake, it's the only thing that matters.
   —e. e. cummings

William Butler Yeats, 1865-1939

# The Bones of My Chinese Name
### by Onnyx Bei

*Shu—*
This is the first stroke in my family name.
*Yéye* arrives in America in search of new beginnings,
but he carries memories of his old life.

*Hengzhegou—*
The second stroke takes a turn with a hook.
Grandmother marries him with the agreement
to raise their children as Christians.

*Heng—*
The third stroke is brushed within the first two.
His first born doesn't learn the order
though the order runs through his veins.

*Heng—*
The fourth stroke sees the birth of his daughter,
but Sunday school occupies her leisure time
like peonies occupy the bees in the garden.

*Heng—*
The fifth stroke encloses the character.
The surname, however, is not complete.
He waits for the next generation.

*Ti—*
The sixth stroke celebrates his sixtieth birthday
with peaches and noodle-filled bowls and the birth
of his first grandchild after a mid-autumn festival.

*Dian—*
He brushes the last stroke on handmade rice paper
saved for me to carry his legacy,
and so I learn the art of calligraphy.

# The Carnival
### by Onnyx Bei

Flashes of light and dark against my face
spin 'round and 'round the carousel—
divine pleasures and mundane sorrows.

I lost a friend who was looking
for a way out of his mothered misery,
lost in his own phobia,
living in a house of mirrors.

He broke his own reflection
until there was nothing left to break,
nothing more than a shattered spirit
for the reaper to take.

I found an abandoned automaton
who gave me what I needed
just when I dwindled with fear of desertion.

She jerked and flashed and sputtered my fortune:
Every silver lining has a cloud,
it's up to you to flip your luck.

Ever since, I return to the Carnival
to ride the Ferris Wheel
and delight in the horizon
when the ride stops at its peak,

where I feel I am close enough
to reach and rattle the clouds
for rain and for thunder
to find my way out of an aching existence—
an overcrowded midway.

# Chronicles of a Forlorn Woman
by Onnyx Bei

## 1. The Language of a Rose

She pushes a threaded needle
through fabrics and daydreams
of the silk and fancy lace
she once afforded.

When sweat reaches her brow,
she wakes to find herself
in a shop sewing faster
than other seamstresses
because the work is not constant
like hunger, like thirst.

She sews to make ends that don't meet
and pricks her finger every time
she threads a needle
hopelessly beneath a dark cloud.

This is not the same America
from her dreams, but
no hablo Inglés
doesn't get you far.

With bandaged fingertips,
she arranges a wasting rose
in a vase near the window sill
crying out for earth, water, sun
in a language of her own.

## 2. Post-Divorce Metamorphosis

It's easier to thread a camel
through the eye of a needle
than to forgive—
and my mother's
metamorphosis begins,

a mother I don't recognize
with eyes that look at me
not the way a mother
looks at a son,

but the way a woman
looks at the man
who consumed her—
thirsting for closure.

She masks her misery,
a hidden dark side
like the far side of the moon,

and I want the far side
to turn and come close enough
for me to touch its craters
and smooth its surface
though the earth may drown,

but we're already drowning
in an earthen dam
damned for our sins
since Adam and Eve's
dismissal from the earth
to which I'll return,

*ojalá*, fulfilled
before she overflows
with madness—

this earth,

my mother,

*tierra madre.*

3. Thorns

In her garden,
she becomes a surgeon

and performs
a horticultural operation
cutting the stem back
to the first three leaf clusters
leaving at least two leaves
between the cut and the stem.

Overwrought with emotion,
she jerks the roses from the root
and crumbles the blossoms.
Her hands bleed,
but her pain is deeper
than the thorns in her palms
and bolder than fallen rose petals,
furled and withered.

4. My Father's Eyes

I cover my eyes which
remind her of my father
to smooth the pain away
as we mend the missing years
the way she mends
her tattered garments.

Yet night racks her bones
and thins her blood
that's thicker than time
and thicker than pain
that turns into hate,
that turns into fear.

I sit like willow branches
in a still night
underneath a red moon
on a rocky shore
and wish for a spring tide.

5. A New Beginning

She brushes her hair

ninety-nine strokes with a trinket
she lost long ago,
and she finds the will to forgive
he who transgressed against her.

The ocean tide rises
to the top of *Cerro Mogotón*

where the ravine-guard sings
on a distant Sunday,
and we plant Mystery roses
recovering our lost time.


# Refugee Camp for Rare Birds
by Onnyx Bei

We sat like eggs in a carton
waiting to be poached.
What was the probability?

We'd wake up to bad news
and scrambled eggs,
hard boiled eggs,
sunny side up eggs,
or potato and egg omelets

when potatoes were available.
That's the uncertainty of living
in a battle zone; we never knew
when we'd have potatoes

and only one thing was for sure—
we had plenty of chickens
that laid eggs regularly,
and we sat like eggs in a carton . . .

All that is history now, at least for us.
But history is like a broken egg shell

in the compost, it recycles itself
with a new cast of characters.

I was having breakfast
when I heard the news
of a bird specialist arrested in Zurich
for smuggling 25 rare bird eggs.

And as I dipped my toast
in the yolk of my egg, I thought
of the many smuggled eggs
that burst from their shells

with red, white, and blue feathers—
the colors of a dream that take wing
across the American sky.

## A Suicide Note
### by Onnyx Bei

A row of rain doves resting on a telephone wire
extending from my home to yours
calls your name.
I regret not calling sooner.
In my coffee, nimbus and mammatus clouds
float from this world to the next.
A note in the grounds transcends time to a place
where the Lady of Shalott weaves a tapestry.
I see your fears a coffee cup too late.
Your fate's been composed
and all I can do is finish the poem.

## Beboppin' to Another Beat
### by Travis Bowles

An all-nighter at The Landing, listening to jazz all alone.
Smoke and neon fill the club with shifting wisps of liquid light.
Wrap my ears in velvet, sultry solo of a saxophone.

Bass poppin', piano playin' while the clarinet begins to moan a solo.
Slowly taking over at first, raising the shady spotlight.
An all-nighter at The Landing, listening to jazz all alone.

Outside the city bustles and hustles. Amalgamated masses drone
on and on and on. Tucked away beneath the cobbled streets, a different
shade of night. Wrap my ears in velvet, sultry solo of a saxophone.

Rocks in my scotch lazily shift all on their own.
15 years is good. Young, dumb, still view the world in black and white.
An all-nighter at The Landing, listening to jazz all alone.

Davis, Gillespie, Coltrane and Armstrong set a smooth, classic tone.
Young, up-and-comers fuse sound, playing with all their might.
Wrap my ears in velvet, sultry solo of a saxophone.

Ashtrays filled with nothing but butts as night fades to mourn.
A couple bucks for the band, just one more song all right?
Another all-nighter at The Landing, listening to jazz all alone.
Wrap my ears in velvet, sultry solo of a saxophone.


# Co-op
   by Travis Bowles

She's got game, but I don't know how to play.
↑ ↑ ↓ ↓ ← → ← → A B B A
Mashing buttons hard enough to break the controller,
Trying to get a high score, but you can't control her.
Aim to please, try to tease, at least equip a smile,
But data's corrupted — can't detect the save file

Wait! There it is : )  ....... Thanks for holding!
Are you sure?            <yes> or <no>         Now Loading...

Things would run smoother if I just read the FAQ.
Don't know what power-up's best suited for the next attack,
Perhaps I'll 1-up myself with a cheat code—
Will it work even on insanely difficult mode?

She's no trophy, but keep playing to unlock an achievement
Even with a Gameshark, I can't figure out the right sequence.

I've been rolling solo so long, but this here is co-op,
And my Player 2 just joined and hit <START>


## Whittling Away the Time
### by Travis Bowles

A seed, a sprout, a tree,
a mighty oak. A branch
fallen; discarded on the ground.

A man of the earth, mighty and old like the oak
finds the branch. Inspecting from all angles,
tossing and sliding it around
in his hands. Testing.

A rocker, old like the oak.
An heirloom in which the man was
rocked to sleep as a sapling.
He sits, branch in hand. He whittles.

Sliver by sliver, splinter
by splinter—seasons change,
crops harvested and pickled
for the coming Winter.

And yet, he sits shaving
away the cocoon of bark.
Watching as the old wood
gradually, painstakingly, transforms
from the deserted limb, one of
thousands, into something new—

A horse, whistle, castle, doll,
flute—no one knows, except
the old man sitting there, whittling

away shaving by shaving,
piece by piece.

Pausing to rock, to enjoy
a subtle fall breeze, admire
the leaves shedding their
Summer coats for Fall's
bright new fashions. The wood
goes nowhere fast,
why should he?


## A Taste of Salt
### by Alaina Bray

He paid for his whiskey while everyone
else bought their gas and water. The weather
man had said cat three. Evacuation
was mandatory. He would've run either
way—always did. His wisps of white hair carried
the scent of failure, his latest attempt
to quit smoking. He thought of the rest: married,
then divorced, an entire life as unkempt
as his hair, hopeless like his lungs, the wards
of smoke and asbestos. There would be no waste
if he didn't stay. He pried the old boards
from his windows, sat and breathed the first taste
of salt, the calmest wind he'd feel that night.
"Now," he said, "now. Let's see me do this right."


## What Was Missing
### by Alaina Bray

My childhood dog, a mix of chow and cur,
had puppies the summer I lost my lisp,
three alive, one still.

I couldn't have known what was in her mouth,
when I went to take it. (Mom and Dad

were good with secrets). She dropped it,
obediently, in my hands. Slick with mud
and saliva, it curled limp against my skin
and curved from the boneless back legs to the neck
and stopped.

I stared at the pink and white of my palms that night
and pressed them to my neck every now and then
to feel the blood flow between my throat and jaw,
trying not to think of what was missing
sinking with unopened eyes into
the dark wetness of her maw.


## Baby Bunting
by Erika Jo Brown

American oystercatcher, American coot,
American widgeon, American woodcock—
the indigo bunting just blows all of those
away. Don't call me a perching bird, says
the perching bird, so help me G-d. Average
in every way, 6 inches tail to tip,
this swift passerine is super blue
in a dun, done world. How can anyone
bring children into this done, dun world?
It's as easy as two plus two. One indigo
bunting and another indigo bunting think
fleetingly of the tanager, of the warblers
returning late night to their nests, drunk
with song. Indigo bunting, bird of prayer,
please stay in the breeding coloration
illustrated in the field guide of American
fowl, or come take refuge with me.

# Garden Stakes
by Erika Jo Brown

I am a fucking plant. I am silent.
Think of it: loam, stone, roots.
Maybe I'm a succulent. A mother
walks by with a waddling infant.
Social scientists encourage lots of
babble during cognitive development
and she's a conscientious mother.
Baby is essentially vegetable-headed.

Mother says, "This is a dandelion.
That is a daffodil." The Babel
of naming enchants a reverie.
She considers the sting of
humiliating bosses, the hipbone
she loved once on a sultry night.
"Bearded iris." Tulips abundant.

"Baby," she says, "you can snap
its head off with your little finger."
She shows him how. This is
her life now, allegiant to her
descendent. She wants him to know
all the secrets of the garden.

I will grow again. Maybe I'll be
another matter with another mother.
Maybe there will be no mothers
where I'm going. I'll go now.

"That's a gardenia. That's a geranium."
she says. "That's a zinnia." She tells
their names, like once, on a summer night,
she gave Baby his always name.
Our names will fill her mouth until
she's not lonely, just like us plants.

# Translation
by Erika Jo Brown

I am translating
a poem. I'm doing it
right now. The writer doesn't
know what people think of her,
not really. Put it this way:
she's a 21$^{st}$ century girl.
Or this way: she lives
near a taco truck so
fragrant little fragments
get stuck to her sweater
and her puppy thinks:
nourishment. How do I
know all this about the
writer? We keep in touch.
Mostly laughs, but I
suspect there is a lot
of darkness on both
our parts. She disagrees
stridently with the simple
diction I use. We wrangle.
In a language with such
exquisite words, like
exquisite or nuthatch,
why keep saying I
she wants to know.
She seems to know
a lot about my language
but she will never really
know how I understand
my language, what it can
do to two people on a balmy
night, and that's exactly
where I derive my power.

# Trench Foot
### by Erika Jo Brown

It may seem inconsequential to you
but I had wool socks and little peds
and athletic socks and intermediate
business socks in the laundry today.
The weather is inconstant. Don't you
miss just staring at a washing machine?
Now vibrating, now humming, now warm,
now industrious? My sorrow is endless
is the name of a song by Cesaria Evora,
chanteuse of mornas. I could never
say such a thing out loud. I could
catalog my laundry. Imagine the feet
of Neanderthals trudging. Imagine
how many foot soldiers were lost
over shitty socks. I hate brilliant
blue days because I am always doing
something stupid. Mr. Sun in the park
with a candlestick. By the time I get
there, the sun is always dim and
it's cold. My sorrow is endless.


# At the Creek, Before Dawn
### by Keely Disman

I stare at my watery reflection,
an outline filled with blackened
eyes, gaunt face. The world is grimly gray

as I stare into yesterday, today,
and tomorrow. Sun creeps over the trees,
coloring the world, and I look into ancient eyes

surrounded by crows-feet, age spots, scars—
years of fisted fear, constant chaos, etched in flesh.
A wren stirs on its branch, fluffing

feathers, chirruping its welcome

to the new day.  The world brightens,
shadows fade, revealing thin lips

which slowly stretch, lifting one side,
then the other.  The woman staring
at me smiles and I smile back. A small motion

infusing stagnation with fresh resolve
and the little wren sings in the sweet gum.


# Butt of the Joke
### by Keely Disman

Windshield wipers thump loudly
on an old pick-up as it speeds by,
sending rooster-tail waterfalls
to soak sidewalks
and hapless pedestrians.

Dull greyness is broken
by a Skittles rainbow of umbrellas,
the flattened blue foil-lined chip bag,
and a yellow binky forgotten
on the concrete.

Doors buzz constantly
as people rush in, out,
clustering under the eaves,
screwing up their courage to run
the obstacle course of rain-drops and puddles
like the girl in the black hoodie,
shorts, flip-flops.

Huddled birds decorate power lines.
A stray tabby dozes on a tire,
sheltered by the fender well.
One valiant water drop
clings to a leaf tip
above the pink-and-white-azalea
blossomed landscape.

Peering through rain speckled glasses—
the world thrown into contrast.
A discarded cherry-red-lipstick-marked cigarette
is swept away on the whitewater rapids,
flowing down the gutter.


## C'est la Vie, Coprinus Fimetarius
by Keely Disman

The night is tepid
as they push up hauntingly
through black mulch,
like a miniature ghost
army invading the flowerbed.

Membranous umbrellas
perched open on slender
milky straws blanket
the bed, boldest
in the open, shyest
peeking from under
the marigold leaves.

As sun rises and shadows
fade, their stems
become elderly, feathery
tops curl, wilt, pull into
themselves, collapse, dissolve
into black ink in the
morning heat. An end
at a beginning.


## Grandpa "Kaw-Liga"
by Keely Disman

Weathered brown skin, laced with fine white scars.
Tobacco stains shade the already dark fingers
long used for holding a smoke.

Wrinkled, gnarled joints hide steel.
Nails trimmed short. Hardened calluses
mark a man used to hard manual labor.
Wide palmed, to gently cradle.
Long fingered, to firmly grip.

Hands that smoothed oil into leather,
sanded rust off metal.
They turned the breach and supported
the shaky newborn foal as it stood.
Tenderly they turned the garden soil
yet ruthlessly pruned the plants.

In the mall, amid the kaleidoscope of Christmas colors
and tornado of activity,
body taut as strung barbed-wire,
tense jawed with hooded eye, his unease was plain.
As out of place as a horse-drawn wagon in a Nascar race.
Arms crossed to barricade him from this modern madness,
he stood in dislocated silence.
Stillness surrounded by whirling chaos.

Distinct in the din, the close sound of crying.
Kaw-Liga woodenly bent down,
gently brushed away the tears,
soothing the lost child.
By the time the harried mother arrived,
young and old hands clasped,
little boy laughter invited smiles from passers-by.
"What are you doing?"

"No child should be lost or afraid, for they carve the trails to the future."


# Making the Front Door
### by Keely Disman

Sawdust tickles my nose with bitterness,
coats my tongue with grit, settles
on the concrete floor like falling snow.

Caustic varnish from a nearby can
elicits a sneeze, and the chewing scream
of the table saw makes me long
for earplugs. Shelves of old
coffee cans overflow with extra nuts,
bolts, nails, screws. All of the drill bits
arranged by size. The ball peen hangs
on its hook by the door. Discordant echoes
reverberate in this drafty, tin-roofed shop.
The table-saw stills, relieving my
abused ear drums, till the hand sander
starts humming. The white oak quivers
during its transformation into the sturdy
defender of my home.


## Melody of the Night
### by Keely Disman

*Inspired by Leonid Afremov's painting*

The night reminds him of happier times.
Greens and purples play peek-a-boo
with the fiery hues of lamps lining the park path.
The impasto of color contrasts
the darkening blue-night skyline,
reflects off the rain-soaked concrete setting it on fire.
On the other side of the canal, the lamps
illuminate buildings that stand like sentinels behind them
and their reflections make the water burn.

He saw the young couple stroll off with their dog,
the man's arm nestling the woman into his side,
their forms turning to shadows
as they walk away into
an azure happily-ever-after.
The dog looks back to watch
as, huddled in his thin coat,
he claims the park bench the couple

has just vacated and remembers a time
when he'd had a family, a dog, a roof over his head.


## A Single Mom Goes Back to College
by Keely Disman

The Tasmanian Devil spins, whirls,
stirring my mind's sleeping form
under its fog blanket;
causing thoughts to scatter, scramble
(like cockroaches when the light
flips on) and hide so I can't find the ones I need.

Lamp desk and laptop screen glare intimidatingly;
interrogation lights in the dark room silently waiting
for answers I don't have; can't seem to find.

Weighted lids and rope-knot muscles
pull me down, protesting the time
and crouched posture.  Churning stomach
pickets the empty coffee cup standing mute amidst
crumpled white pages, empty Red Bull cans, and a bruising
scatter of blue and black pens, green and yellow highlighters.

Black spider letters crawl across the page
refusing to stay in comprehensive order.
The blaring alarm clock plays the Jeopardy-themed
count down of my remaining time.

Burbling gurgles fill the quiet room
and that blessed aroma draws me slowly,
achingly, from my chair, mug in hand.
The bitter brew teases my brain
into some semblance of awareness.

Furious clicketty-clack-tapping produces
final answers.  Save.  Print.

Test a shirt from the pile in the hamper
(good enough), pull it on.  Shimmy
into the nearest pair of jeans
(never-mind the mustard stain from fixing lunches).
Slide on the worn-out tennies.
Grab the precious white stack off the printer
and shove the paper that is my class final
into my tattered back-pack.
A quick reminder to the kids not to miss the school bus
and I speed out the door once again
to resume the chase for a higher education.


## The Summer I Prayed for Rain
by Keely Disman

Inside the tiny house, chaos reigned.
The noise of the air conditioner valiantly struggling
to keep the heat at bay and failing.

Children squabbling like mutts over last night's scraps.
Arguing about the TV, the radio, toys, the least little slight.
Patience is the memory of winter snow

and melts away in the heat just as quickly.
Tempers flare and scream like a boiling tea kettle
as temperatures rise inside to match those outside.

The walls close in; claustrophobic on this summer day.
Escape is out the door into the barren waste outside.
Not even the hint of green to relieve the brittle browns, dusty yellows.

The smell hits before the heat, setting fire
to the nostrils and now watering eyes.  Death, decay,
the stench of rotting things coming from the checkerboard

of muddy brown puddles that used to be the blue green creek.
Not even a thought of a breeze to provide relief.
Eyes search the blue bowl of the sky in an unspoken plea to the heavens.

Above the barren tree line, a bank of dark clouds tower.
Will prayers be answered?

Breath held in anticipation.
                    Watching.
                                    Waiting.

The faintest whisper of rumbling teases the ear.
A brief caress of air across sweat drenched skin.
Hope stirs.  Another rumble, a firmer caress.

Like the battle cry of charging men,
the wind roars to life, filling the air with dust and debris.
Blowing the smell of death away and replacing it

with the smell of mud and the promise of life.
It carries the black clouds on its back as it races onward.
Lightning flickers in those dark depths like foxfire

with the occasional streaking brilliance of shooting stars.
Clouds race in like a thundering herd of buffalo to blanket the sky.
And then, like a white wall, the rain comes,

marching triumphantly across the parched earth.
Cooling.  Soaking.  Saturating.  Life-sustaining.
The children step outside and watch in awe

the stately progress of rain across the yard.
Thunder now mixes with squeals of delight and laughter.
The rain washes tension away as easily as it cools our heated bodies.

Adults and children alike, drop their façades and burdens
to play in the blessing of rain.


# Tainted Love
by Keely Disman

Muddy snake
slithers across white skin,

tracking its life path
in winding patterns.

Needle pricks
and Sleeping Beauty
fades into nightmare.
Venom burns the dross
and innocence to ash.

Sun burned lungs
struggle to function
as the body eats itself
from the inside—
mind, heart overwhelmed.

And the frog prince
watches, waiting
to feed off her kiss.


## The Botany of Absence
by Jason Duncan

The labor of trees is shade,
but when we buried her
my brother and I rode
down streets abraded by daylight.

Green chains knotted the roadside,
each stalk a headstone for seed.
As the casket lowered,

light as pollen,
St. Augustine stiffened its blades.
The earth fell in

and we threw cut roses.
Beneath our feet roots fought
to turn less pale,

groped the mineral dark
for a fresh hollow to fill

tapped the planted skull
for memories of wind and past rain

and drew the dead up through stems
to carve a single, broken bloom.


# The Creation of Loneliness
by Jason Duncan

Sitting alone in a white-washed apartment,
one wall a mirror to make the illusion
that emptiness doubled isn't emptiness after all,

my mind turns to God
and what He saw in the beginning
when the Spirit moved across dark and silent waters.

Were His eyes affixed on a rippled, black reflection,
the shade-visage of the Almighty
silhouetted in endless absence?

Did He utter the Logos in a whisper,
as if to himself or to no one at all?
And when man was made in His image

was it that of the Father cloaked in light
or the solemn titan who alone
knows the body will unlace to dust?

His hand must have paused
over each atom of iron
in the furnace that forged our blood,

fingers arched to form the heart,
the lungs, the entrails

stitched together with veins
into an effigy of the eternal.

Outside my window
night stains the sky,

while street lamps flicker on,
one by one, as do the stars,

despite the void between them.


# Ghazal of Burning Silk
### by Jason Duncan

"Music filled the ground where the Sultan's five wives took the air. ...
Guests had to dress in clothes that matched the tulips (and avoid setting
themselves on fire by brushing against the candles carried on the backs of
hundreds of tortoises that ambled around the grounds)."
—The Tulip, Anna Pavord

You sing, breathing fire and smoke that speaks your name
your voice a burning bell that melts from light to flame.

Tulips wear your ashes, a gown of shattered moons
while stars unstitch the night and drift from light to flame.

Swaying in the garden a row of broken blooms
the hue of bloody snow that turns from light to flame.

You are the Sun's mirror though fairer even now.
His hands glide slowly through you and twist from light to flame.

Your bones will unravel and drag along the wind.
The breeze will seek a sea that glints from light to flame.

The world is an inferno, the pyre of your flesh,
and dawn sears through the living, a flash from light to flame.

My palace is a tower built of dust and shade.

Its halls lead to Jahannam and wind from light to flame.

I, Sultan Ahmed, own each branch and stream,
but cannot clutch your soul before it flares from light to flame.


## Neurology
by Jason Duncan

How does it all begin,
the skull as an opaque killing jar
of beauty?

Somewhere a branch bends in the wind,
and a spark arches through the cerebellum,
axons flung like the constellations of a mad astronomer.

How does it all begin,
a jay shrilling out in the sky's same hue,
the tympanic sea growing silent
until the memory of pecked figs and sunlight
crescendos into consciousness?

Or the scent of house wine and cigarettes
and the single tear you dabbed into a black napkin,
the amygdala wrung dry as a raisin
but still straining for the serum of grief.

How does it all begin,
the snake coiled in St. Augustine
that turned thalamic fire into the sudden regret
you had not seen the year's magnolias bloom?

Or when you lay all day by the glass skin of a creek,
stones tumbling lazily through the stream
like so many signals floating through ganglia.

How does it all begin,
limbic, cortical, mammalian?

In the end synaptic sparks have done
as much to fill the bone with light
as stars that strive to dream of day
while cloaked in endless night.


# Pica

by Jason Duncan

I dreamt last night of swallowing stones,
river-rounded, bright as glass

and awoke choking on the mineral weight
of the imagination.

As a child I once chewed the spiraled cap
off a sand castle to taste the grit

of the shore, to fill my belly
with the shells and the salt and the soaked

horizon that proved there was no difference
between the sky and the sea.

If only it were so that a handful
of Saint Augustine could be chewed,

digested and the whole of young
summers amid magnolias
would return, that to devour bees
would mean a throat full of honey.

If guzzled ditch mud would infuse the blood
with joy, bring back the dead

and stretch the night sky of '93 anew,
I would drink down every silted ounce

and remain thirsting.

# Shoot for the Moon
## by Theresa Ener

1.
dont mind me.
im *nobody*.
thats what my mama say.
i dont believe her.
mostly.
coralee, git yer head out that book
git out there and feed them chickens!
im learnin, mama!
dont you want me learnin?
learnin fer fools think they can be somebody.
you a *nobody*.
you wrong, mama!
im gonna be somebody.
just you wait.
put that dang book down, girl.
do yer chores.
mama dont like sass.
she like books even less.
i love mama,
but she sure is simple.
aint got no dreams.
i got lots of dreams.
 big ones.
i sure *am* gonna be Somebody!
one day.
2.
i go to the fifth grade.
at the harvey maines elementary school
over in jessup.
i ride a big school bus sos i can get there.
i used to walk to the pine woods elementary.
they close that place
when the mill burnt down.
all the people move away.
all the children gone.
cept for me.

and my friend cracker jack.
hes just third grade.
hes the only friend i got.
those kids at harvey sure can be mean.
they dont like me and jack.
say we white trash.
and stupid.
jack aint too bright.
but i try real hard.
i do good.
thats what my teacher say.
miss carters the nicest lady in the world.
she give me gold stars.
mama say gold stars is for fools.
but i know better.
3.
i love my desk.
its my very own.
miss carter put my name on it
right across the top.
coralee james.
with gold stars.
she know i like the gold stars.
fifth grade is the best so far.
i wanna go to fifth grade forever.
miss carter say no way.
she dont know the real truth.
the bus aint gonna bring me to sixth grade.
sixth grade over at the jr. high
way over in cyrus.
twenty more miles down the road.
too far, they say.
so fifth grade gonna be it.
mama say nobody need learnin
not past fifth grade.
but miss carter say shoot for the moon.
i aint too sure what that mean.
but it gotta be a good thing.
so i reckon to figure it out.
4.
bein poor aint easy.

but we dont do without.
not really.
cracker jack aint so lucky.
he dont got no daddy.
just his mama and old pappy.
and baby gray.
she the prettiest baby i ever saw.
skin like dark night.
eyes blue like the sea.
nobody know who her daddy is.
dont matter none though.
shes a blessing.
thats what mama say.
mama and jacks mama is best friends.
have been since they was little girls.
i wish gray was older like me.
we could be best girlfriends forever.
but i got jack.
he aint so bad.
we do fun stuff.
and he listen to all my dreams.
dont say a thing bout me bein a crazy fool.
he say mama the fool.
i say, hush your mouth, jack.
mama just simple.
plain as that.
jack say he gonna marry me one day.
aint no way.
i sure do love jack and all.
but not like that.
we like kin, me and jack.
people dont marry they kin.
not if theys smart.
thats what my daddy say.
5.
my daddy cry when i was born.
thats what nanny james told me.
he cried?
cuz i was ugly, huh?
jesus, child, no!
he cry cuz he was so happy to see you!

you was a miracle baby.
a miracle baby?
like jesus?
oh, lord, you a mess, coralee!
see, the doctors told ya daddy
he wont have no children
cuz of that dang war.
he was hurt real bad.
they say it messed up his parts.
i dont know nothing bout daddys parts.
thats his business.
but i sure am glad i was born.
me, too, sweet baby girl.
you the light we was all needin round here.
mhm.
i like bein the light.
makes me feel like Somebody.
6.
i dont like my name much.
it aint pretty
not like those girls at the harvey school.
sometimes i tell jack to call me mary
or susie
or kathleen.
he say he like my name
just the way it is.
my mama name cora colleen.
she always go by coco.
my daddy name leevelle.
so thats how i got my name.
coralee.
coralee imogene james.
my nanny james name imogene.
shes so proud i got her name.
i aint got the heart to tell her
i dont like it even a little.
i just keep that to myself.
shes a sweet nanny.
she like my gold stars.
7.
may on the way.

i been wishin time to slow
let me be fifth grade just a lil longer.
wishin is for fools.
time just tick tick tick away.
dont care nothin bout coralee.
i aint ready for schoolin to end.
i just aint ready.
miss carter ask me why i mope
and look so sad all the time now.
i told her my old dog peanut done died.
i dont know why i told the lie.
i aint got no old dog peanut.
i got the kitten name scat.
dont want miss carter worryin bout me.
wont make no difference no how.
i just gotta figure it out
how can i do this shoot for the moon.
all by my lonesome.
maybe i ask miss carter
at the fifth grade graduation day.

8.
the rain aint stop for 13 days.
daddy say the crops gonna float away.
mama say that aint funny.
this serious business, leevelle!
how we gonna make those ends meet
if we aint got no crops?
oh, coco, stop that hollerin.
we been through worse.
all gonna work out just fine.
mama dont buy that hopeful stuff.
shes a prayin woman.
but she aint got the faith.
nanny say mama turn her back on the lord.
mama say he had it comin.
grandmama smith pass on
when mama was a lil girl.
mama left all alone.
i just might turn my back on the lord
if he done take my mama.

girls need they mama.
9.
may come round.
i aint none too happy.
i sure aint feelin like no light.
mama dont got no sympathy for sadness.
git on up and git yourself ready for school!
dont be lazin.
i wanna go.
i really do, mama.
but my heart is sure a breakin.
girl, you just put that sad business out yer head.
life go on.
that for sure.
but mama, i love the school.
learnin make me feel special.
oh my jesus,
we aint put on this earth to feel special.
we here to do our work.
i dont wanna do no blasted work!
i wanna keep learnin!
coralee, you try my patience.
jesus tryin my patience, mama.
yes, he is.
10.
cracker jack aint been feelin so good.
i gotta ride the big school bus
all by my lonesome.
i keep to myself.
dont ever look at them other kids
who stare and laugh.
people just wrong sometimes.
even young people.
shame on em.
thats what my nanny say.
shame on they hateful hearts.
but why they gotta be like that?
why they gotta make fun?
i aint dirty and stinky.
my mama scrub me down most every day.
no child o mine gone smell like a pig, mama say.

dont matter none, i say.
they gonna poke fun cuz they mean and spiteful.
shame, shame on em.
11.
i was missin jack.
mama say i can go for a visit.
that aint no easy task.
his old pappy aint kind,
like my pappy.
my pappy done pass on bout five years ago.
nanny miss him sorely.
he sure was a good man, she say.
aint none finer.
thats the truth.
jacks pappy like the drink.
he sit up on the porch sippin
from dawn to dusk.
jack stay outta his pappys way.
i cant say i blame him.
drink make a man ornery.
but i was bound to make my visit.
cant no cranky old man keep me away.
12.
jacks mama saw me walkin up the road.
she come out to greet me.
look who we got here!
coralee, you lookin something beautiful today.
thank you, miss lilah.
jack round?
yeah, he layin up in the bed,
moanin and a fussin.
he be happy to see that pretty face.
i brung him a book.
think he might like it if i read a story?
i been practicin.
oh, he love them stories!
you go right on in, girl, and spread that light.
dont mind pappy.
he nappin.
she smile and give me a teeny hug.
and a pat on the bottom.

miss lilah know how to make me feel like Somebody.
13.
jack got the chicken pox.
he look like a big polka dot mess.
i tell him so.
that aint funny, coralee.
i been sufferin mighty!
yup, hes in a fussin mood.
men act like they dyin when they sick, mama say.
women gather theyself and git on up, she say.
we got work to do!
men, they moan and fuss.
jack aint no man.
not just yet.
but he sure on his way with that belly achin.
i got my work to do.
gonna do my best to cheer his spirit.
nanny say i got the gift.
must be that miracle light jesus done give me.
i sure am grateful.
14.
i was happy to be sharin my stories with jack.
even if hes bein whiney.
i brung tom sawyer.
hes one crazy boy, that tom!
always in some kinda trouble.
me and jack get in troubles of our own.
his mama laugh and tell us behave.
my mama dont laugh.
she send jack on home and tear up my hind end.
that tom drove poor aunt polly up the wall crazy.
i bet *he* dont get no whoopins.
jack sure did like those adventure stories.
he said he would be toms friend,
if he could.
you can do adventures with us, jack say.
if you wanna.
sure, i say. i would like that very much.
jack is a tried and true friend.
for sure.

15.
i was glad jacks pappy still nappin.
i tiptoe past, just to be safe.
he dont scare me.
i just aint got no patience for drinkin old men.
they oughta know better.
my pappy never touch a drop of that alcohol.
he was a god-fearin man, my nanny say.
daddy dont do much drinkin.
once in a while he pull out the jug
when company come by.
mama dont mind much.
she take a few sips and act real nice like.
they might even take a twirl.
me and daddy do the twirl now and then
when he aint too tired from the field.
he used to cut a rug, mama say.
i dont know nothin bout rugs,
but daddy sure can twirl.
im learnin.
thats what daddies is for.
to teach they girls how to do the twirl
and whatnot.
16.
next week is big graduation.
mama say she makin me a special dress.
nanny help, too.
i hope they make it blue.
blue is my very favorite color.
blue like the ocean.
one day im gonna see that ocean.
its in my big plans.
daddy say he will get me there,
somehow.
im gonna build sandcastles
and dip my toes in that salty water.
daddy say he gonna catch fish.
i aint ever had no fish.
mama say its the best thing she ever did eat.
cant be better than chocolate, i say.
nothin better than chocolate.

its *my* very favorite of all time.
17.
well, the big day finally here.
mama get me up extra early
to fancy my hair.
i aint keen on it, but i oblige.
nanny say i look like a lil doll.
i dont know bout all that.
but i sure am lovin my new blue dress.
mama say she use special fabric
from a dress she wore back in the day.
she did good.
it fit me real fine.
daddy come in from the field
to see me off to school.
well, coralee,
you the prettiest little princess i ever did see.
take a twirl for your pop.
i do a spin around.
i got that big silly smile.
i sure do feel like Somebody.
18.
im so glad cracker jacks all better.
i dont gotta ride that bus
all by my lonesome no more.
hes waitin for me when i get to the bus stop.
he look at me like he done lost his mind.
geez, coralee, you sure look nice, he say.
why, thank you, jack, i say.
today your big graduation day?
yup, i sigh.
this for sure gonna be a happy/sad day.
coralee ,who gonna ride the bus with me
when you aint goin to school no more?
dont you be worryin bout that, jack.
you gonna be just fine.
i aint got the heart to tell jack no different.
i sure hope those harvey kids aint mean to my jack.
he aint tough like me.
poor jack.

19.
me and jack is the first kids on the bus.
mister donny, the bus driver, nod his head
like he always do.
he say, you are a sight to behold, miss coralee.
i figure thats probably a nice thing,
i smile real polite and say thank you, mister donny.
jack like to sit in the middle of that big bus,
right on that big hump where the wheel go.
its jacks turn for the window,
but he step aside and say, go on ahead, coralee,
its your big day.
i get to watch the world go by.
the sun comin on up.
i lean my head against that window and sigh.
my cracker jack always do such nice things.
maybe he got the light, too.
20.
them harvey kids see me sittin there
in my new blue dress.
they stop and stare.
i stare back.
what you lookin at, i wanna say.
but they seem almost nice like.
they see me different.
but im still me.
just me in a pretty blue dress.
aint no different from me yesterday
or day before.
im awful glad they aint bein mean
on my one special day.
but they ought be nice all days.
maybe they treat my jack nice when im gone.
i sure hope so.
he aint done nothin wrong.
so i smile real big at them harvey kids.
they dont smile back.
but they aint laughin.
thats a good sign, i think to myself.
and i reach over and give cracker jack a little pat.

21.
that big bus pull up in front of harvey maines,
and i feel a dark cloud creepin over my heart.
this the last time i gonna be here.
last time i gonna see miss carter.
lord, that make me sad.
i give anythin to be back at first day of fifth grade.
do this whole year all over,
start to finish.
but god dont give no do overs.
you get one shot, daddy always say.
i got my one shot.
just move on, my mama always say.
but i feel stuck.
my behind is stuck in that bus seat.
i aint ready to get this day over.
i just *aint*, lord.
why, oh why, cant wishes come true?
it aint right, lord!
just aint right, i tell ya!
life aint fair, coralee.
life just aint fair . . .


## Nake nula waun welo
by Donna Finney

Like the balloon that hovered over Emerald City
as rumors of gold in those Black Hills ran rapid
that fateful expedition,
suspended in time.

Orders from Grant,
"Ride 'em up. Drive 'em out.
Into the reservation with them! I'll send
The Squaw Killer."

Grown men,
anxious as bird dogs awaiting the first shot on a duck hunt.
The lucky 7th cavalry,

600 troops,
marching,
led to Paha Sapa,
sacred Black Hills,
land of the Sioux.

　　　Little Big Man.
Thought you would capture
innocent women and children,
outsmart the Red Man and lead them to you, once more?

Napoleon's glory was in your eyes,
praise heard in your head.
Visions of attacking a small village,
but the waters of Little Big Horn River
saw your blood instead.

Sitting Bull inspiring his own vision.
A surprise.
Two great warriors,
Crazy Horse and Chief Gall.

12,000 Sioux and Cheyenne yelling,
"Nake nula waun welo!"


# As Best I Can Recall
### by Casey Ford

I.　　The Age of Things

My first time here, I'm struck by architecture
America fakes, too young to understand.
(The *Wiener* tour guide says it "kyoop-a-la."
In Texas, I believe we say it wrong.)
We're singing folk hymns inside Matyaskirche.
A heartbeat out of time, the organ roars
to keep my mind here, but I'd rather be
sitting in a slender pew to marvel
at old-world things, the crypts of saints and kings.

My slim heel catches the uneven floor;
our voices soar, sail through rood and nave,
joining the choirs of centuries ago,
which, with fewer notes and simpler hearts,
entreat us not to squander time or sound.

## II.   A Bus Tour of the City of Music

Too busy singing—no time for walking tours,
so we mostly saw the city from above.
Rain-streaked windows kept us from the light
shining through the Habsburg's regal town.
Mozart, we miss you, but I have a hunch
today we'll do *Hosanna*. Be with us,
our footprints set in these—gigantic, timeless.

We pass by an apartment; Strauss—it's yours.
Some stories up, you wrote the waltz we love,
*an der schönen blauen donau, kalt und breit*.
Would you cringe to know that now this building's down
to a McDonald's? Would you stop for lunch?

Not to speak of Schubert! (No, not from a bus.)
Next stop, Salzburg. *Wien*, we knew you thus.

## III.  das Licht

"To piss where he pissed!" all the boys would say,
too cute to own the awe, the ache that pulls
us inward, jaws ajar and hearts aswell,
hot to tap into the muse here—Mozart's town.

We toured the castle—nice enough—today.
The Alp outside my hotel window cools
my room at night. My dreams of Mirabell
made real, the tulips stretch to my lean down.

Yet nothing else has moved me quite this way,
like the remnant spirit of the savant fool
that lingers, not near tomb or dank stairwell,
but in the airy veil he wove around

the town, symphonic tapestry of light
pooled in, draped on all that's left in sight.

IV.  Confession

We pace, sightseers, come from near and far,
about the old town square. Old men play chess.
The astronomical clock's apostles tread
the hour, each hour, when death has chimed the bell.
Young men hold hands, and cafés serve their beer.
Nearby, on the Charles Bridge, a star
marks the place they drowned his tortured flesh.
Five steps from the saint's stone, straight ahead,
it's here the truth unfolds. From heaven or hell,
the martyr, John of Nepomuk, will hear
confessions of daytripping, giddy pawns
for one brief touch, a hand on hallowed bronze.

It starts to rain. An old man lifts his dear
grandson's tiny hand to what, for eons,
has been a nucleus of saving grace.
Grandma snaps a picture. I am here
admitting that my faith has offs and ons.
I pray to John as rain rolls down my face.


# Offices of the Wraparound Porch
### by Casey Ford

I.    Matins

The moon, highest in the sky,
sings its silver song.
My eyes closed, I am awake.

II.   Lauds

Owls hunt at the witching hour.
Would-be victims flee—
darkness offers no shelter.

III.  Prime

Dawn. Horizon pink, fiery.
Sunrays peek through stars—
percolating coffee drips.

IV.  Terce

I'm baptized in tears;
leaf, stem, and grasses dried of
dew, the grief of dawn.

V.   Sext

Straight up and straight down,
the clock's hands, the sun's warm rays
remind me: look up.

VI.  None

Naps. Hot dreams in brief,
vivid. The swing sways, the chains
creak like ancient gates.

VII. Vespers

Cicadas call for sunset;
sheets flap on the line.
I pray to quiet Heaven.

VIII.   Compline

From here I see the highway;
headlights, streetlamps, specks
of fireflies' phosphorescence.

# Shoreline Devotional
### by Casey Ford

In silt and tar,
on sticky brown waves,
knobbly, pungent
mounds of sargassum,
dense air salty, thick—I think how
a future we claimed so resolutely
is not the one we got.

I'm standing in it, on the shore of it,
in shifting sand and saline wind,
certain I've found the spot—
the very ridge in the dunes
where the world opened wide
from the back of your F-150,
our rust-ravaged marriage bed,
legs tangled in your mother's blankets,
wild hair, electric skin, frenetic hearts—

Twenty years gone,
treading this gray Gulf strand,
digging in with my toes,
I unearth repressed ache
for those kids
that night
on this beach,
and tonight
at water's edge,

accompanied by moonless stars,
sighing waves, and sleeping gulls,
I sing, for everything unborn,
a prayer that this sand's memory
holds on to what I could not keep.

# Thirst
by Casey Ford

Drought allows for sifting through the past.
Lake levels drop; the Sometimes Isles appear,
grow large, reveal the campgrounds of the lost.
Bits of old boats, tents, tin cans, dead trees,
upper cretaceous footprints in the clay.
Peninsulae develop by degrees.
Ephemeral, they'll drown again someday.

Some writers' pages fade from black to gray
just as these isles will vanish with the rains.
For some it's true—*omnes insulae,*
we isolate. Our words run out like blood
and water, but our legacy is wrought
in memory or in the acrid drought,
when Earth is gasping, thirsty for the flood.


# For Kathryn
by Emryse Geye

*tulips.*
open mouths
red, yellow, purple, pink
hungry for the watery sun
that meanders down
through the February freeze.

we push from slumber,
wiping dirt-covered eyes,
escaping our tombs  and
both begin to hope.

*two lips.*
i open mine and
breathe your names,
take your long string—

shining like polished gold—
and pull it from my throat:

it tugs at me, hooked in
my gut, sewn in
my flesh and tied in
my veins.

i choke on the sound.
i kiss you and swallow you.
i push you towards my toes.

we bloom, expand, progress, and peak.

until i can blow you out,
lips ragged and aching.
finally remove you from
my bones,
my thoughts,
my tongue,

in a cloud that
shimmers
before it fades.


## The Landing of the Whip-Poor-Will
by Emryse Geye

Mother's father comes home
and we help him from the car;

he will be dead within the month

and that silence echoes in our throats.
Flesh melts into my shaking hands
as his body tries to slip from my grasp:
legs and arms and terrified eyes and
I am struggling to hold on.

Who decides to draw hearts like this:
two halves, like two teardrops ready to fall?
Like asking for trouble, like stepping on cracks?

The hospital shirt comes up
and the sallow, marked skin shows through—
I can see every vertebrae straining;
hollow bird bones aching
to fly, to be free, to leave
all of this indignity behind.


## New Orleans
### by Emryse Geye

Sometimes, I peek between
the window and the driver's seat
to see his hands contract on the
steering wheel: laced fingers
cradling this journey

the transient landscape
and his passengers, as they sleep.

Sometimes, I wish I could
feel his forearms twist like
ropes behind my back
with fingers like fence posts:
territorial and tempting.

Sometimes, I remember the
midpoint, the apex, like the
fold in a piece of paper:
if I stand on the edge
we can still fall down.
I remember him turning me
over like a page of poetry—
a reminder of his desire and his fear.

# The Recruit
## by James Johnson

One, two three.
One.
The musty odor of decades of pain rushes into
Your nose as you lower your chest closer
To the sweaty floor. You push back up
Only to see five perfectly aligned fingers thrusting
Towards your face. The anger of
A grown man leaves the Smokey Bear
Hat and smears itself on your soul.

One, two, three.
Two.
The itch on the back of your neck
From the haircut that morning
Is overcome by the fear running down your spine.
The tears of the recruit to your right scream regret.
The red pigment on the cheeks of the recruit
To your left radiates inability.

One, two, three.
Three.
Your muscles quiver as you continue moving.
The promise of honor is your fuel.
The aura of pain is your ignition.
Exhaustion hangs on your back continuously.
Your mind can't organize a thought long enough to miss home;
It is preoccupied with the frog voice in your ear.
But you're the one who signed the dotted line.
This is what you asked
Four.

# Boats Against the Current
by Mercedes Kelso

### A Response to *The Great Gatsby*

A beautiful little fool I once was
Though now I walk through the valley of the shadow of death
Past the ash heaps, past the eyes of the omniscient man who sees all
Poised, sophisticated, and charming, but cynical I have become
For bliss is found in ignorance
Not the trembling coldness of an artificial happiness
So I stride on, going through the motions of life
As the clock ticks on
But you beat on, boats against the current.

A generation lost in power, lies, and drunken carelessness
We traverse the scandal of dishonesty, selfishness, the American dream
Only to discover the false illusion of an absolute little dream
That will be sought for but never tangibly held
For the party is over and the corruption prevails
As the clock ticks on
But you beat on, boats against the current.

Young love we once had
Passionate, breathless, glowing
And elegantly irresistible
Transforming a rainy day to one with radiating sunshine
But isolated and extinguished the day has quickly become
By a disappearing hope that will quickly vanish
As the clock ticks on
But you beat on, boats against the current.

So I remain, saddened by your beautiful shirts
Understanding the fault in carrying well-forgotten dreams from age to
age
And you, tricked by a single dream for an authentic love
Fade into the ashes
For you can't repeat the past
"...Of course you can," you say
But a false hope this is

Shining as a green light in the distance
The glimmering shreds of the past
Waning by the second
As the clock ticks on
But you beat on, boats against the current.

The well-forgotten dreams from age to age can only be carried for some
time
Until taken away
And we remain, lost in the cynicism of reality
Desperately seeking passion and meaning
In an unforgiving, broken, and distraught sea of hypocrisy
As the clock ticks on
But you fade into the eternal abyss of ashes
Hopelessly forgotten.


# The Bridge
by Mercedes Kelso

A Response to Ito Romo's *The Border is Burning*

The bridge that spans the red river
Divides two worlds.
A group of men lingers outside of the Southland Café on one side
And on the other sits a little old woman on the bank
Grinding mulberries into a dark mortar stone

Dangling from her wrist, the shiny beads of her rosary
Glisten against the desolate soil
Holding the prayers of a forlorn life
Her hands cracked and wrinkled from years of scrubbing dishes
Gently touch the smooth grooves on the mulberry
From the banks of that red red river,
She watches the water flow downstream
Carrying the memories and sorrow of a life of struggles

The mulberry tree grows tall on both sides of the river
The strong scent of the berries blending with the hot, muggy afternoon
rain shower

Pouring over her frail frame,
Into the red red river,
And onto the unforgiving asphalt
That bridges the gap between the two worlds.

She sits and watches the generations pass by
As she grinds the mulberries into a fine dark red powder
A passage once undisturbed with people passing through as they please
Now a center for turmoil, violence, and chaos
With only the familiarity of the strong scent of the mulberries enduring
in the warm sticky air

She softly touches the beads on her wrist,
Watching as the fine mulberry powder seeps into the red red water
Flowing under the concrete blockade
That bridges the two worlds
Never to be closed.


## Dead Flowers
by Mercedes Kelso

A Response to Toni Morrison's *The Bluest Eye*

There were no marigolds in the fall of 1941.
The storm arrived
And the meaning and sweet nostalgia
Of a lifetime that could have been full of laughter and bliss passed along.
The passion and creativity of a childhood
Robbed from a youthful face
Born innocent and beautiful
Into a world that tells her she is ugly, dirty, inadequate.

Holding a piece of untouched natural beauty in a cruel world
The marigolds grew bright and dazzling
Against the bleak background of an unforgiving terrain
But after the apocalypse of the blue eye they no longer grew.

An idealized society
Dick, Jane, and Shirley play on the freshly cut lawn

Behind the gate of the white picket fence where the hollyhocks grow
While their mother
With pearly white teeth, ivory skin
And the bluest eyes, with a glare so cold,
Stares at our ugly skin that we cannot seem to scrub clean.
So we peer from afar
Only hoping to one day be accepted into the repulsive but alluring magic
That sits beyond the glistening white picket fence.

Though the nature of subordination is cruel
To sit and watch amongst the dead weeds and dandelions is now our
only desire
For the marigolds no longer bloom.
Had I planted them too far down in the earth?

No, the marigolds were not planted too far down in the earth
But the build-up of years of hatred and discrimination
Rest deeply ingrained in the roots of our legacy.
Only to fuel us with the desire for revenge.
So the marigold seeds remain sterile and trapped
In the dry, callous, and merciless soil.

The storm arrived
And like the perpetually hostile cycle of life
Certain seeds the earth will not nurture
Certain people humanity will not love.


## My Private Hell
by Mercedes Kelso

What I call the struggle of humanity
Is a dark world of turmoil and sin
Anxiety, insanity, never ceasing

For I dwell in a desert of my own kin
With a mask hiding my inner fear

I can't pretend that I don't grovel
In self pity, so shallow and vain
Guided along by the dark apostle

We unfortunate poor roam the street
Moving closer to the fiery hostel
To the purr of the long black train

Haunted by loneliness I continue to search
Only hoping for completion
That two roads might converge
At the golden steps of blissful eternity

This seldom but genuine heart of hope
So bleak and unattainable
In a world where darkness lives only to cheat

False promises entice and tempt
Winning the battle between purity and corruption

I am saddened and tainted by the brutal fire
By the cynicism of reality
An ever so harsh world in my living Hell.


## The Earth Mothers
### by Jennifer McFarland

Like ancient trees, they choke the lesser weeds.
These pregnant wives, these alpha moms—they rise.
When into shallow pools they birth their seeds,
they petrify while cradling their prize.
Their hollow, bloodless wombs, once fertile loam,
soon fill with earthen minerals: the clay
with which they mould a perfect little home.
They clothe themselves in husks of brown and gray.

And I am just a tree, with seeds to sow.
Watch every autumn; see my colors flare.
I drop my leaves.  I harden in the snow,
and from their shadows, angle in despair.

Come spring, I'll leaf, and stretch my branches high
to soak a scrap of light up from the sky.


# Involuntary
   by Jennifer McFarland

It's like the moment after
crashing, when you feel
for blood and broken bones,
push the airbag aside,
try the latch
and escape.
And the other driver emerges,
shaken, blinking, bruised,
but seemingly whole.  You meet
on the pavement, exchange
information, assess
the dented panel,
the tire-tracks snaked on the road,
the dangling mirror.
Of course, you both deny fault
and his denial makes you
question your own involvement,
so that as you drive away
the tears begin to rain.

Or it's like waking in the morning
with a certain heat, a certain
wetness, hair disheveled,
nightshirt slipped
from one shoulder,
but with bright eyes,
and a feeling that if
you reached, you could

almost remember.
A curl of dark hair.
A hand slipped downward, and up,
A hot, violent rush.
But no, your mind dwells
on the alarm clock,
the morning traffic report.
The memory strains,
so you have to drag the ebbing dream
to even drudge up the hair, the hand.
And nothing more.

More like a feeling
in your chest, your arms,
or just behind your eyes,
almost suffocating, almost breathless,
almost hyperventilating.  Or rather,
beyond the primitive need to breathe.
The smell of static air
at sunset, the rose-pink glow
at the horizon.
A feeling that if you close your eyes
and stretch your arms
and hold your breath
     just so,
then maybe you can hold it
even for a second, grasp it
before it slips away.


## Weekends with my Husband
### by Jennifer McFarland

He straps on a backpack
holding fifty pounds of lead weights.
I wear light, absorbent clothes;
a cotton tank top, a bandanna to mop my brow.
This is no romantic stroll in the park,
but his so-called death march.
Eight miles over grass

and concrete, past the water
treatment plant, hiking
on the sides of roads. The fields flowering
with candy-bar wrappers and trucker bombs,
plastic pop bottles
filled with yellow-brown liquid,
stewing in the sun.
We reach the death part,
an iffy stretch where the road's shoulder
disappears, the sports cars
and Texas trucks doing thirty over.
A bridge crossing a wide swale,
and a lull in the traffic entices me
to run for it and leave him behind.
My stride lengthens, my blood pumps
truck exhaust as the end of the bridge
bounces closer, closer, and then I'm doubled over,
my head spinning on traffic fumes,
my lungs bursting.

This is our chosen recreation.

On vacation, we don't sunbathe.
We wade into Lake Michigan
on a red flag day.
The sky is gray, the water black,
clumps of weeds churn on the surface.
The waves swell over my head
as we press on to the second sand bar.
I clutch his hand, fearing
we will drown out there, together,
certain we will drown
if separated.

A wave tears my fingers from his
and I scramble for an instant, desperate
to find his hand again.
I'm pulled under and can't tell which way is up
 until my head smacks the sand
and I'm churning like a weed
on the bottom of the lake.

And just when my lungs feel as if they will burst
I find the floor, push up to the surface.

My husband is still standing
on the second sand bar, searching
for me, stretching his hand
as I shout over my shoulder and over
the roar of the water
that I'm through,
and paddle like a soaked dog
back to the shore,
and sit on the cold sand, watching him, panting.


## Ennui in Mission, Texas
### by Charles McGregor

I didn't want the Whataburger to end my night, but gas station merlot
    couldn't keep me home.
 Instead, I blink at loitering boys with puffy jackets bouncing on the
    hoods of cars
as they wink and nod at a stout girl with a checkered scarf. She raises
    her lip and snarls
through her nose. They shove her shoulder and break her coquettish
    pout.
My gaze is broken
    by a lachrymal man as he walks
through the W shadow
    sniffling and heaving down a dark road.
I follow him.
    He winces
at the touch of his left shoulder.
    "What's the matter?"
He shakes his head not comprehending what I'm saying. He walks on
    and I feel
like he wants me to follow. A lust for confrontation,
knowing all my possessions are locked away,
    propels me forward.

In the darkness the earth clicks and croaks at the lachrymal man and me.
A pale orange light gives us a glimpse of a small house made of
     damp wood. Next to it
is a field of neatly plowed columns. Clouds of bugs hover above creating
     a new troposphere around shrubs I'll never name or plant. I want to
     be in that world
where I'm in possession of calloused hands
     and a damp house.
Grandma Figueira rocks in a wicker chair
     and points at me.
"Ennui! Ennui!"
     I can shake my head.
"No, Grandma. No ennui. See?"
     I present my hands as proof.

My smile is broken by the lachrymal man's rough hand
     guiding my lower back towards a gray minivan. The shards of glass
on the driver's seat manifest in ultraviolet nano-flashes. The lachrymal
     man heaves
and reanimates the scenes with elastic waves from his right arm. He
     ends
and assumes I'll provide him with a companion answer.
     I nod and smile.
He becomes distraught
     shaking me hoping he'll rattle out the correct response.
I frown.
     I am afraid.
Then he sticks his pinky and thumb out putting what is left of his fist to
     his ear.
     "Cellular! Cellular!"
I shake my head.
     "No. No."
He groans falling back into the van. I shrug and look back the way I
     came.
Grandma Figuiera will be there on my return journey. I tell myself
*just be polite and wave.*

# Grandma's Ft. Myers Beach
### by Charles McGregor

*1. You just know*

Grandma smiled like an alligator. Her charcoal skin
filled with chocolate cherry sun spots
greeted you every summer on her wooden patio.

You can fancy Grandma all you want. Go
to the beach shack. Feel
the sea breeze steal up your nose. You
cannot touch her anymore.

*2. You dream*

You believe that Grandma is a three-hour drive down Alligator
Alley. Along the way ashy cane polls
dip into the highway waters of the Everglades.

"Take off your clothes, Bruno."

Grandma is prepping you for the beach. You loathe
the greasy lotion and her slimy hand waxing your body. You are
annoyed, but don't realize you shouldn't be.

*3. You walk with Grandma*

The beach is not far. You should
exit the pebbled driveway,
take a right at the house
with the peeling Geo Storm,
pass the 7-Eleven
with prism colored Slurpees,
cross the two lane street
in front of the pastel souvenir shops
with the puffy shark floats
standing erect
in the hemp baskets. Then you will
smell the saline wind,

hear the waves crash
and feel the bleached sand
scorch your feet.

*4. You feel Grandma in the ocean*

Grandma opens her folding chair and sits
atop the waning dolphins. You spread your towel
and sit beside her sipping an off-brand
of diet orange soda. The sun tickles your skin.
The sun stings. You escape

sprinting into the ocean with Grandma
by your side. She floats
over the Gulf of Mexico
while you swim under her head
and come out of her feet
blowing bubbles along her back because she says

"it feels like a Jacuzzi."

Your legs slide across her butt and thighs
before you gasp for breath above. Her skin
is tender and thick as the blubber
of a rubbery porpoise. I would
willingly touch her only under the Gulf.

*5. You never want to see the sun set*

Most of the time we would
leave before the tangerine sun
would set over the moldy pier
to our right. She
wanted to stay. You
wanted to go. We
hardly ever stood
long enough. You
just didn't know. You
didn't know.

# Merlin's blue hat
### by Charles McGregor

bent over in strawberry fields
while I lounged in a wicker chair
and felt pale.

Stained baseball caps
and Merlin's blue hat
stood up and bent forward, stood up and bent forward.
I sipped lemonade
in a wicker chair
and felt pale.

While the cool porch
with Spanish tiles
was making more
lemonade, I strolled
towards Merlin's blue hat,
felt conversational and asked:

*Do you enjoy your work? Do you like picking strawberries?*

She didn't understand. I ran
back to the porch.
I felt pale—parched
for more lemonade.


# San Antonio Displacement on the River Walk
### by Charles McGregor

A cardinal hops down the stone steps. It leads me to the brown river
   failing to
turn plastic green.

A big ebony man kisses the neck of a white female in his lap. *Go on
   through.*
*Nothin' is stoppin' ya.* I accept his invitation.

A white baby girl runs to the river to meet a floating Mallard. Her dad
    snatches
the bag of brown pellets. *One at a time. The ducks will get greedy.*

A golden girl with a pink backpack is startled when I brush by her.
    Pieces of
ripped Cypress Tree bark—a currency I am unaware of?—spill out of her
    Ziploc bag.

A big man in a cowboy hat bows to a Helen of Troy next to him. *Well,
    you're*
*gonna spoil me now, ain't 'ya?*

A golden girl in a white wedding dress walks barefoot across the stone
sidewalk. She complains about cold feet to the girls lifting her train.

A lesbian couple holding hands bumps into the golden bride. They click
    their
tongues winking at me as they pass by.

The golden bride climbs atop a stone staircase. Her eyes look down at
    her big,
illuminating hands.

A silver haired woman sits next to me on a concrete bench. I hide my
    bridal
magazine. I tell her where I am coming from. *Oh honey, you're a long
    way*
*from home. Thanks for visitin' anyway.*


# Turkmen Wealth
### by Charles McGregor

*I. From Bazaars*

I left you a West—a hero worship of American wealth. We
walked and I audibly cringed at clay roads soiling my pink feet. You

did the same in mock disgust. You pointed to the bazaar. *Pepsi. Coke.*
*America good, yes?* A gulp of the Pacific Ocean and my

America—it tastes the same in Cyrillic script. I dreamt in waves
of familiarity. Then you tugged my sleeve and pointed. *Dog sick.*

A rigid mutt foamed from the mouth. Its eyes could've shattered into
        marble
shards. We kill misery in America. You call it sick. I felt

privileged then. Missed privilege then. Your mother told me *America*
        *good.*
*Turkmenistan bad.* I gave a sympathetic no. She shopping list-

-ed an answer: *Computer. Television. Big House. Car.* Ya'll wanted
photos of America. I presented big fish at aquariums swimming in their

obvious beauty. Ya'll nodded disinterest and asked where my house
was. I said I had no pictures. I said it was small. Ya'll asked

where my father was. I said he died penniless and sad. Ya'll gasped
*wa-hey*, clicked your tongues, and warded off the evil eye.

*II. To Mansions*

I wanted to carry the dog at the bazaar away. I could've taken it
on the next flight and shown everybody how ya'll

live. A frothy, rigid dog life—a humorous anecdote. It would
make a fine lawn ornament. Once America grew boring again,


I could fly my house to Turkmenistan. I would have big furniture.
A big television. A nice car. A mansion with a rigid mixed

breed watching out for the evil eye. Of course, you could live
with me. And your mom. She'd like my big house. I could feel wealth

in front of that bazaar. Not present in our moment, I shook my head.
        *That poor dog.*
You dropped my sleeve and scowled. *He not poor! Don't say that!*

# aunt beryl
by Grace Megnet

collections   of   easter
eggs from exotic places
trunks full
her  second  husband
gambled  and  suffered
from            epiphora
widows  believed   him
lost
she  tore  old    tissue
papers  in dark  rooms


# I AM
by Grace Megnet

Here exposed like everyone
not I this one
light of the world

Not a taxidermist afraid of John Wayne
A Black woman
So distant from the hope of myself
with you always

Beggar of the world
bread of life
From the dirt under the back porch
I am—yet what I am none cares or knows


# Ostbahnhof July 2014
by Grace Megnet

bristling with pink tennis shoes and untied laces
frozen lattes and coffee they call with crema
sun glasses in lemon, orange, and checkered
lots of pictures in color now, remember

79

the water still flows but
how different it was
grey
I remember the dogs, the dogs


## Top
by Grace Megnet

calm at last
i feel my brain
outside the window
all the leaves
hang empty
only one
each time
i breathe
like magic
swirls
weird thoughts


## Finding the Search
by Matthew Mendez

I find myself in that moment:
Where I have put myself to discover,
Where I know I
have found it before,
In a place with few disruptions,
Yet a spark I hope will find me.
I go there for quiet.
I go
there for the soft sounds.
I go there to hear something.
Is it only inside me?
Each
leaf is a story.
A tree describes the forest.
The wind sings it best

In various melodies.

The sun and moon pour through.
Nature waits and was there before me.
I rediscover also
what I did not know:
What to look for.
I want to be amazed.
If I can only let myself be.


# Tikkun Olam
by Matthew Mendez

Vibrant skin of
The taut canvas
Modulating translucence
Evocative spatial modalities
Warmly fade into
Evaporative awe
Belle haleine
Plentitude of rich actualities
Thread of beguilement
Expectation and introjection
Hope idealized, internalized
As Humanist joy
Grow, relish, enjoy
Functional sweetness
Hyperactive hum of light
Instinctual playfulness
Emergent phenomenon
Generous illusions of
limited conformity
Penetrative celebrations
Reconstituted objective identity
Material intimacies
Alternative integration
Secret of redemption
Creative reparation

# Undergrowth Paradises
### by Matthew Mendez

Suggest the creation of a perspective
                    that numbers the interpretations
                              upon the viewer involving
one's own reflexion process
a contemplative iconography
motifs architectonically constructed
pointilinear layers as a surface
curve away from the attendant figures
who digitally excavate aspects
inviting audience actualization of meaning
forging new contexts that
                         resist ossified criteria
juxtaposing knowledge derived
from personal allusions
engaging cultural phenomenons
escaping entrenched aesthetics
a liaison to true editorial engagement.


# I Only Worry Occasionally
### by Bryan Owens

that the boy who lives upstairs
will kill himself or his family one day
& blood will run into my apartment.

Right now all the leaves like little fires
have formed cliques at the lip
of every driveway & still the shredded

Valentine's balloon up in that pine is hilarious,
but what has me down on my knees in slippers
is all this glass like dangerous microscopic diamonds
scattered over the cobblestones of my back porch.

This boy needs an exorcist
or a good teacher because his father is in jail

or dead or in Atlanta with some other woman's kids
& that's why the boy kicked out
the window last night.

I let my students watch Dead Poets Society
as a kind of Christmas gift before finals
so they can see what an inspiring teacher
looks like & when something bad happens
the good teacher always takes the fall.

What would John Keating say? stepping out from the green wallpaper
to lean on the staircase;
would he impersonate
his way into the boy's heart?

Would he quote Whitman & say
*Re-examine all you have been told at school
or church or in any book, dismiss whatever insults
your soul, & your very flesh shall be a great poem.*

Maybe it wouldn't work on this kid,
but I spend my days off picking up glass,
& later I'll tell others how terrible it was
though really it's not.

When I'm done I'll put holiday lights overhead
in the canopy of branches
& all the shards that I miss
will shimmer like angels in the dirt.

# Poem in the style of Coach Greenshield
### by Bryan Owens

When the Lord fashioned the cock
like a magician revealing a wand with his fingertips,
it was preordained that Coach Crandall,
fresh kineseology graduate, hide his junk
like an impotent worm in his basketball shorts.
He likes to brag to his friends about going to work
in basketball shorts, but really coaches needn't wear

basketball shorts, I mean we're doing more
than blowing our whistles here, but coach Crandall
with his monkey ears & needlepoint skull
likes to get in the mix with pubescent girls,
blocking shots or playing the elbow game
on the soccer field & each time I see him
with groups of girls at lunch huddled around him
as he twirls his whistle,
& the inside jokes he keeps like various
little tops spinning throughout the school,
I think oh Coach Crandall you sorry douche bag.
& a wave of cutis anserina spreads across my back,
goose flesh, I mean, which is a question on the Health final,
but that it feels like sprouting wings of resentment is not,
& how gratified I am with myself
shaking my head when I'm out of his sight,
saying Lord help this kid learn to go home
gladly to his loneliness
so he can do his job.


## Symbolic Sarcophagus
### by Bryan Owens

The objective of the Symbolic Sarcophagus Project
is to bury bigotry once & for all.

In your lecture, sarcophagus from the Greek means 'to eat flesh,'
that's why limestone,

believed to decompose bodies greedily,
remains the best material for the job.

The students vote to throw Christ in there,
pull him down like a Christmas tree in February.

But Christ is dead already, so to earn an A,
we must consider those whose minds are small

like an appendix that is septic & refusing to rupture.
Those, that is, who fail to transcend the identities they've inherited.

So you mean we can bury Tony? Katie Bowman says
gesturing to the boy in back of every classroom

who tags 'Thug Life' in sharpie on the desk.
In a few years he'll shoot a rival gang & miss & hit

two girls playing together with sand in their hair
in a sexless kind of playground lovemaking.

I think my mother, says Brenda,
belongs in the sarcophagus too,

for wasting her youth dreaming a wedding
to wear a dress so extravagant

three bridesmaids held the gown
in a London Hilton bathroom.

Now our house is a shrine of wedding photos & little
plastic bottles of bubbles with wands in the shape of their initials.

If there's room, Michael says,
Maria Camila, Victoria Consuela, & Ana Sofia all

take prenatal vitamins in Mr Zarniak's 1st period.
I thought someone's water broke in the hallway

but it was just a spilled Ozarka & photos from the sex party
get reposted on Instagram every #ThrowbackThursday.

All manner of lowlife stereotypes exist, you say,
so each student must contribute at least one. Come who has another?

My cousin, says Cory, had four children
at the age of 21, used welfare money for drugs,

locked the kids in a closet with an iPad,
disowned them one year, moved across the trailer park

to live with another woman & take care of her kid.
He got shot in the back when SWAT raided his heroin operation.

Yes, you say, bring them all in on Tuesday.

The morning of the project you bring donuts.
The students arrive with CVS materials purchased at 2am,

& set to work building a sarcophagus around the bodies
piled in center of the classroom.

When the students slide the lid in place, they request
you lie on top for the papier mache mold.

Now the students are finishing the donuts.
As you dry, you can only listen to the interred clamoring to get out.

They are trying to break through
& this last-minute bullshit will not do.


## To inspire them
### by Bryan Owens

I tell them reach for the stars.
I tell them it is due Monday.
I tell them turn off the lights.
I tell them what it's for.
I say 'skeletons.'
I tell them listen to your heart.
I tell them that is bad writing.
I tell them Declan got his finger stuck
so the pencil sharpener no longer works.
I tell them to search for the passage
I have already marked with my thumb.
I tell them it's not appropriate
to ask a teacher about kissing.
I tell them when I was divorced
I very likely was destroyed, but
I have let others break my heart since, so

you see, I was not defeated.
I tell them great things have modest beginnings;
except the life of Christ
that was epic pretty much start to finish.
I tell them the best kiss ever
happened over a pepperoni big slice
& a cold glass of milk.


## What Lasts
by Bryan Owens

With neither family or friends,
a former student & I split a beer.
Sitting on either end of the couch
we watch the ball drop on an old Zenith.

Blue light curls up
like a cat on his scalp
where an incision has healed
in a pinch.

The beer is coconut curry hefeweizen
& I can't bear it.
In seconds he drains his glass of all but webby foam.

I fall asleep shortly after midnight
& dream he tiptoes by to steal
what is left in my glass.

I wake up,
this sofa is not mine
nor the blue morning light chalking
its way across the room
& all its matter.

The glass of flat beer
that is still full...
That is mine.

# When I Was Jesus
by Bryan Owens

The new principal outlaws students & faculty
from dressing up for the day on Halloween.
& I don't care, I'm too old for it, but I flip on the tv
& they're crucifying Jesus again.

I was Jesus one Halloween. Ms Gratzer
told us dress up as historical figures
that inspire us. So I was Jesus on the bus

with a bread loaf I finagled
from a La Madeleine display & a beard
I waited to put on at school.

Kurt Cobain put me on the spot,
& with the whole class watching
I recite nearly 6 commandments!

*Look everyone*, says Gandhi, the train
of his garment draped over his arm,
*Ms Gratzer came dressed as a terrorist.*

*No, class,* Ms Gratzer says, *I am Mary
Magdalen.* Her face is covered
but she looks at me
because I am Jesus & we evidently
had a thing way back then.

I see Jesus in the boys' bathroom mirror,
washing his hands a million times
using the soap dispenser somebody has punched,

& Van Gogh left a reefer smell
in the handicapped stall so principal Spencer,
dressed as principal Spencer, searches me in his office.
Parting my robe, he finds no paraphernalia taped to my thighs.

At lunch I wander to 40 classrooms looking for Lunch Bunch Bible
    Study,
multiply the chili dogs & wear a hairnet with the lunch ladies,
eat lunchables with Merlin, Archimedes, Harry Potter, & Hedwig
where I copy the notes for history class.

The Joker's cheek flesh is ripped to a smile
& she pulls me into the stairwell before final period,
holds hard to the nails in my palms

when sexy Darth Vader comes down the steps
clutching a math book in her arms, says,
*sorry, didn't know you guys were in here.*

All I can say is I remember choosing my costumes each year
to be an elevator for the self,
to take cover & rise & declare

I wish to be different in these ways.


## After the Accident
by Adrian Patenaude

Take out the stitches
and conceal your scars.
Don't wear the sling.
Insist on dressing yourself:
button the blouse,
inch into jeans
and struggle into shoes.
Don't let them see you wince.
Type with one hand
and microwave cold pizza.

Go back to class.
Smile brightly.
Refuse to mourn.

Pretend you don't need painkillers.

# ars poetica
### by Adrian Patenaude

a poem is potent
distilled & aged
like fine wine

a poem is breath & voice
the same spirit moving
both beat boxer & string quartet

a poem is a black dress
classic & timeless
the color of mourning

a poem is truth
the whole truth & nothing
but the truth

so help me god

# Brethren
### by Adrian Patenaude

It's August, but a June bug,
black almond on legs,
scuttles across the stage.
We rush out to squash it.

Unthinking, I snuff out a pixel-sized bug,
a life-force crawling on my computer screen.
I conceal the body in a tissue grave
and sanitize my hands.

On the news is a funeral of bees,
an accidental homicide with insecticide.
I recoil at squirming cockroaches
like a beggar without fingers.

Buddha said a human soul
dwells in a cloud of mosquitoes.
Distracted, we swat
at ancient brothers.


## Golden Hour
by Adrian Patenaude

I walk barefoot across the narrow board
over softly flowing water and step
onto the cool, muddy berm.
The rice is the gentlest green now,
thriving in deep, delicious mud.
Soaked in rainwater,
the paddies reflect evening sky
as bits of sun escape rainclouds.
Green spreads out to the edges,
touching the feet of encircling hills.
A scruffy yellow dog catches my eye
as he sweeps by, sniffing
his way into messy water
and snapping at a startled toad.
I sense snails as big as apples
nestled in inches of mud.
The rice is growing tall, elegant,
striving upward like its ancestors.
Before long it will be gold, ready
for harvest, stooping under its burden,
but for now this is enough.


## I Wonder
by Adrian Patenaude

A clump of cactus clutching the corner of an abandoned blue roof. I drive
by and wonder when it climbed up and how it finds food and where it
draws water and why it decided to live that way, clutching the corner of an
abandoned blue roof. Does it miss its cousins back in the old cow pasture?

Will it ever return to visit, long enough to regret life's inflexible trajectory?
We retrace our steps, but even the sky has changed.


## The Scent of God
### by Adrian Patenaude

The scent of God is forgotten, like the aroma of wine supplanted by
grape juice, impotent in plastic thimbles.

The visceral God is forgotten, replaced by softly lit portraits of the
ethereal Christ, the innocuous Lamb.

The swift knife is forgotten, slashing the sacrifice, throat draining red,
warmth caught in rounded cup

and dashed on the altar.
The limp body raised on sticks for skinning, entrails salted and burned.

The fiery spit is forgotten, flawless lamb roasted, fragrant flesh torn by
hungry mouths.


## The Family Name
### by Brandy Rains

Standing in the doorway
full battle rattle:
dress blues, worn boots
knapsack, saggy eyes,
muffled bed-head


I can't help but think
you look so much like our father
whether drunk on American spirit
or alcohol I'll never know

but the difference between you and him
is that you can't sleep

because of what you saw in Iraq
and he can't sleep

because of what he did at home
and the warzone he made of our bedroom
the grenades he hurled at Mom
that made you into a soldier

before you polished
your first pair of boots
and stepped into the sands
of the eastern hemisphere.


# Golden Delicious
### by Brandy Rains

Our sorry excuse for a refrigerator
was a big silver box of electric disappointment
nothing was ever inside it
maybe a bottle of Ranch or two, expired,
yellowing, taunting. A rank steak
from the last time you picked me up from school,
14 days to be exact. Of course nothing
nourishing was ever to be devoured
in our house.
But, somewhere deep in the drawer
hidden under heaps
of goopy green spinach,
shining yellow in its drawer like a fairy-tale,
I found the lonely
Golden Delicious apple.
Robust, round
full-figured globe, a healthy body I'd never seen.
Not once was this apple employed
in a morning turnover, or baked
in a cinnamon Christmas pie,
or smothered in peanut butter.
The same apple slow-ripening in the cold
through my whole childhood or, see above,

the last time I saw you 14 days ago.
Maybe it wound up here from the purse of that new  girlfriend
or the old one
or you bought it because the doctor said
you have to start eating healthy
but you don't want to so you left it for me
to give to my brother
to split with me for dinner?
It was beautiful
but we never ate it
because ten days later when I saw you again
the electricity had been cut off in your house
and the apple had turned from yellow
to orange
to brown
and I told you the house smelled bad
and never saw you or that apple again.
But sometimes, in my daydreams,
I imagine the sweet slice of gold
pressing against my lips.


## Spinning Gold
### by Brandy Rains

I am every calorie I ever burned
and counted that made my fingers colder
and you are every freckle on my shoulder
stretching over and claiming the bones
making mountains through my skin.

I am every hair dismantled from my scalp
dry and faded fate reminding me
that we're all getting thinner here
in the form of a fur-filled, once-tight bra
that used to keep my bones in place,
but the days dragged on
and the lace that shaped my chest grew thin.
We're all getting thinner here.
and thread by thread

94

and hair by hair
I unraveled.
for every bathroom I searched for after
eating a whopping 133 calories
and for every time my mind gave my stomach five pounds
after half a spoonful of rice

and for every time I cried
as a single leaf of spinach slid down my throat
and for every time my eyes fit an entire cafeteria
into a single pit of an olive

and for every time that pit swallowed every vein
that gave me another chance to try again at dinner
and whispered to every sinew,
"We don't need you here."

but you – it's you and that damn hair
that cling to my skin
show your face in my shower
because just as the hair rappels down my vertebrae
and gathers around the drain to make a mockery of what I cannot keep
you run your fingertips across my collarbone softly,
trailing the tresses that cast webs over every dip in my chest
and when I pitch the baggy black tent
for the valleys in my skin,
you harvest every blonde hair with gentle gardening hands
sprouting to remind you that sometimes

you can see all my secrets on my sleeve.
but we all have secrets here.

and just when the dawn breaks through the glass
to define by light that you and pillows
were made to fit in the cracks of my anatomy
you unwind the fading gold strands that in the darkness bind me,
tangling themselves into my pillow
through warp and weft,
with the spindles of your fingers.

It's you. You and that damn hair

that slip your fingers into my pockets to remind me,
"We're all hungry here."


## Gator Song
    by MacKenzie Regier

*Everglades, early 1900s*

The hunter knows the gators sing
the most in mating season, spring-
time melodies he cannot hear
but feels resounding in his ribs.
Every moonrise brings
their deep bass bellows
in the rivers and the ponds,
brings his wife's cold turn
from him as he leaves
their barren marriage bed
to find the scaly sirens, end
their love so loud it makes
no sound and still drowns out
his own. He hasn't heard his wife
since spring began. He hasn't
heard his wife since their baby
was born dead.
               Before
his poleboat runs aground
in a weft of trees, he feels
the ripple-shiver of her call.
He does not see her babies—
black-and-yellow-striped
like winter sawgrass—until
he gaffs her jaw. Her throat
thrums once, they scatter, gone
before his axe has split her scales.
He returns at sunrise to his wife
and does not hear the gator song
but feels it. She rises

from the puddled sheets,
her dawn eyes opening to slits.


## House Sitting
by MacKenzie Regier

      You're not here for me
to ask you about the license plates
sheltered in the silverware drawer,
or why some light switches
operate nothing. A picture in the study;
you, buzz-cut, hair growing in patchy
like a newborn. You're holding up
a gleaming silver fish. The lens
fractures on the bright river,
and at first I do not recognize you.

Water delivery has not come. I smoke
a cigarette from a pack of Camels
tucked in the cupboards next to a set
of dark blue bowls, an empty mousetrap,
then strip my mouth with the last
of the cranberry juice. On occasion,
beyond the window's vision, a distant
basketball smacks pavement. Where
      your flick failed, ash fringes the desk.

Fridge-pinned, a photo of a woman.
Her smile splits lipstick, coat big
against the winter. You must be holding
the camera. I know you by your shadow,
silhouette. Maybe where you are
now, you're taking pictures of her,
a half-melted snowball clutched
in her red glove.

      Cold slinks in
through the cat door, and the grates
blow tepid air. A cobweb, only visible

once steamed, hangs in the shower corner.
You must not have seen. I leave it.


## Non Parlo
### by MacKenzie Regier

In an Italian fitting room, surrounded
by candy-bright panties and B cups laced
with foreign tags,
the shopgirl
traces my shoulders, my belly,
the simple parting of my thighs.

Sticky with English, I try to tell her
I don't know what I'm doing here.
My consonants hit corners, my arms
lie limp as my flat accent. Her hair,

a soft cursive, slides each curl to the next.
Her eyes, ringed in last night's liner.
Finally, her hands. She grants me the power
to stop speaking.


## Two Legends of the Dismal Swamp
### by MacKenzie Regier

Robert Frost sits amid the yellow touch-me-nots
at shoreline and does the opposite,
hands threading vines of muscadines and gardenias,

devil's walking stick with blackish berries,
thorns snagging at his fingertips. It's night,
and finally, he sees them, the maiden

and her lover in their pearl-white canoe.
Just that morning on the train up
as he planned his suicide, he'd thought

how lovely, before he went, to see
not a ripple or a weed disturbed behind them.
And now he thinks of dying

in this soft place—where the silken fog
lies close to the lake, where the silt
would swallow him in its quiet billow.

He wonders if he walked into the mirrored waters
would her lover pull him into the canoe,
would her vibrant hands burn the moisture

from his brow? Suddenly, a whippoorwill,
the arguments of frogs from everywhere. She's gone.
She's foxfire, a trick of the gaseous peat.


## The Skeleton Dance
   by Sammantha Rodriguez

As I played with my dolls,
I could feel their presence.
Those skeletons in your closet.
Watching, waiting,
For the right moment.

Infatuated by my playful imagination
They wished they could present themselves.

Their eagerness overcame you.
Their calls echoed in your head
And finally, after years passed, you opened your closet
Revealing all of your skeletons,
Lined up in a row.


You danced with each one.
Swaying, attempting to place life into their cold granite bodies.
Addiction, depression, and the rest of their friends,
You dance with each and every single one.

And as you twirled and embraced each one
I couldn't help but still adore you.


## The Land of Disappointment
by Erica Saucedo

You want to see the waves of rolling grain,
But instead you see urban blight and trashed tenement.
You want to see the clear, blue world surrounding us,
But instead you see dark mounds of waste.

You want to see the future graduating with high degrees,
But instead you see the future struggling to pay for a degree.
You want to see strong, independent women,
But instead you see men laughing at women for their appearance.

You want to see the land of opportunity,
But instead you see a long line waiting for welfare.
You want to see vibrant, healthy, happy people walking down the street,
But instead you see chronically ill, premature people rolling down the
        sidewalk.

You want to see neighbors visiting each other,
But instead you see kids shooting at a family's house.

You want to see an African-American man holding hands with a white
        woman,
But instead you see a gang of kids beating up a boy for being pale white.

You want to see a young boy helping an elderly woman across the street,
But instead you see a young girl being raped in a dark alley.
You want to see the land of the free and home of the brave,
But instead you see the land of the suppressed and home of the
        cowardly.

## The Dragon
by Ashton Secundino

In the simmering light before the black abyss
A fiery demon kisses the dark like a long missed lover

The glinting of her emerald eyes glow low in the mountainside
Her glittering red scales quiver in the coolness like a shower of silk upon
    skin
Her quick warm breath thickens as the horizon swallows up the
    remaining life of day
Her monstrous wings fill the sky as she roars to life
Cloaked by the sparkling night, she raced onward
Releasing her angst with the beating of her wings
Excitement pumped through her veins
Smoke curled around her vicious snout
Quickening the pace, she hurled herself into the welcoming abyss
Losing herself, she cried orange dangerous waves
They rolled into the night, daring any creature to rise against this
    ferocity
She basked in all her glory
Nothing could stop her
She dived along the skyline
Capturing the night


# Revoltura
    by Genesis Senteno


En el border los elotes no saben igual.
The white mayonesa used to glide with
calorcito from the sun. Calorcito that makes a tortilla
de harina rise on the comal.

Fresas con crema, rojo rosita
like the pink we have inside.

Cuerpos of cabrito
Hanging on the windows
of La Fogata.

Doña Meche said
black caravans stop
in the pueblitos outside of Matamoros.

I see them
Chamacos, escuincles, teenagers.

With a cerveza Corona in one hand,
una pistola in the other.
Grease from papitas sabritas
on their Ed Hardy t-shirts.
Bejeweled cacuchas.

They think they're Americanos.

Their clothes look like the segunda, la pulga.

They line up all the men
hombres de todas edades
como perros in line for food.

"O le entras o te mueres!"

You're out you die.
You're in you will die.

I can hear the disparos

truenan, crunch.

Cacahuates japoneses
with salsa botanera.


## Rose Petals on Top, Full of Dead Bees
### by Genesis Senteno

Dear convicciónes,
that suffocate skin like scum on a coffin,

"We hold these truths to be self-evident,
that all men are created equal.."
y porque no menciona a la mujer?
Men and women are one.

Uno solo.

Are we equal when she's
in labor for 10 hours?
Are we equal when
reckless driving
is blamed on her gender?

Tell me why we women
are ardently told to
be quiet.
Guarda silencio mija.
Calladita te veas más bonita!
A la fregada if you think women look better
sitting down
escuchando majaderías
de los hombres.
Obeying.

Every month you make me remember the sin of Eva.
La manzana. El arbol prohibido.

Don't cross your legs in public,
don't wear short, tight, revealing clothes,
don't incite men.
Everything you do entices them.
No estés a solas con alguno de tus primos,
don't wear red or black clothes.
Colors of desire, passion, y del Diablo-
y no vas usar tampones,
eso es solamente para las mujeres casadas o sueltas.

Burned tortillas, sopa china quemada
trading in those cooking lessons for graduate school.

Explicame porque a man is praised if he has women after him?
Why do you label a cheated woman as a cualquiera?
Algo tuvo que haber hecho.
Ella se lo busco.

MTV videos,
half naked body-esque women
grinding, rubbing
against everything|everyone.

Mis queridas Mujeres,
don't go out to buy the latest diet pill
don't go out to buy the new see through shirt.

JLo jeans to add bubble to your butt,
Victorias Secret push-up bras
(chinhuetas – you won't look like one of those
lingerie models in stilettos just by wearing them),
hours, money
spent in hair salons
painful treatments at Bella Kara
depriving yourself from foods
to fit into a jean size.

Is it enough
to be valued by being 'sexiest woman of the year'?
to be insulted, as wanting to be 'domesticated'
an 'animal, baby, it's in your nature'?

Forgive me Pablo Neruda—
your stories about the body
are full of
abejas muertas.

*"Cuerpo de piel, de musgo, de leche ávida y firme.*
*Ah los vasos del pecho!*
*Ah los ojos de ausencia!*
*Ah las rosas del pubis!"*

# Lull
by Huma Sheikh

The metallic coffee mug
smear-dappled
 a sunburned-stippled face
 of a woman, somewhat upright
 on a white desk across the empty
 pink water bottle, lapped
 in few dew drops—reflections
 lucent soot, scarce and partial.

 The glittering January Sun
 in Canada, a semblance
 of summer in winter
 barren branches, snowless
 streets
 incandescent
 blooming sprouting minds.

Leaves, lush green, fresh
woman's desires, a beautiful *flicker*
icy *slow* trickles
 paradise lull.


# Soulful Moments
by Huma Sheikh

 A shade of beard
 loosely clung to his smooth
 left cheek.
                    If just I could caress in my hand.

 The tasseled out residual fleck
 nuanced sparkles—
 desired uncoiled.

 The hard knuckle dabs over his closed eye lids
 glasses on table, immersed in thoughts—

the conversations, their merger with time.

I wished a moment's clock—
its lifetime.
The soulful melding,
desires for endless tickling—
  locked in time,
  hands swearing continuity
                    Yes, if just.


# Walking close at your side
### by Huma Sheikh

Walking close at your side
In my boots, the sweet,
Rich fragrance of your bare chest, wet
From winter desires,
Clings like crystal strings on my mind.

                          A dire fire

That shines beauty
Make roses of words
The saccharine fragrance


The gentle rustle of hands
Like autumn's
Vermillion foliage
In winter's floral breeze—

Bodies merged
No air
Between
                    Only the sky's sheen

On the winter.

# American Atonement
by Gabe Shulman

*"I can tell the wind is risin', the leaves tremblin' on the tree"*
— Robert Leroy Johnson (May 8, 1911-August 16, 1938) an
American blues singer and musician

Someone get a harp,
*Let it ring,*
*Let it ring,*
through the halls of glory.
A hound on the wayside,
his tongue out,
saliva drip drop.
An untrusting look,
scared is all.
Dust covered cowboys walking
in the hot sun,
like white silhouettes on a field canvas.
There is no storm coming today,
the storm is sleeping in Zeus's stomach.
Dry, dry, dry as a bleached bone.
No hope for no rain.
In spite of it all,
the ground still holds its mouths open
in cracks of expectancy.
Barbed fences hold cows,
scent of blood in the soil,
buried torment,
angry past shaking upwards.
We have made mistakes here;
cities burned,
churches full of corpses,
heads hung from trees.
Fell down on my knees,
went to the crossroads,
fell down on my knees.

## Assis dans le Café
### by Gabe Shulman

West Broadway just outside—
shining in the glow of hundreds
of windows, all trickling down the
sun's light to the street.
Outside—motors, diaphragms,
the clatter of construction
the general hum of all the matter
sitting on top of itself—
Dynasties upon dynasties, risen from
ashes and layered sediment, subway tubes,
artery pipes, granite hearts in concrete shells.

The door blows a cool breeze,
stirring up the croissant and latte air.
The nook embraces its patrons
and the people are comfortable
in the womb of the building.

A drink of latte and dreams
of Romans in red capes, riding
white horses.

Too late, damage done, the tongue
is burned.

The ruckus, chatter, louder and
louder, until my thoughts are
extinguished.

I look out the front for comfort.
A man walks up from the sidewalk
and reaches under a bench next to the entrance.
He pulls out a glorious red apple
from a box underneath and crunches into it.
The bench and box I hadn't
noticed upon walking in.
Perhaps it wasn't even there until he

willed it into being, or perhaps the city
only lets its habitants—
those privileged enough to be in her care—
see her fruit.


## A Daytime Picnic
### by Gabe Shulman

stretch out my flesh
a banquet raw
for the opaque carnivores

blood slowed
like honey ooze
until drank up
with maws and
jarred mandibles

colloidal eyes
(the centipede's delicacy)
soon to be narrow holes
where sockets sprout
little ferns

glistening slugs
will emerge

from the ends of my fingers
elongating the hands

and maggot sanctuaries
will pulse from the core
the birth of a thousand flies
millions of spanning lenses

jackals hunched over
my vessel
picking at bits

to eventually
leave the frame vacant

a sapling spire
leaves unfurling
roots reaching out
coming through the centre
of my being
and into the light
of the midday sun


## Lousy T.V.
by Gabe Shulman

Sitting atop the foundry a crow gazes
down upon a smoking land, barren of desire.

A man walks down his street, knowing death
might be hanging out on the corner that day.

Millions of light years away a star dies
and is tearing a hole in the universe.

In fields of ash and slowly dying
fires, embers glow orange by night.

Newly formed species lie slimy and
stillborn upon the banks of the Nile.

A small boy holds an AK-47, smiling
and aims it at his sister jokingly.

In the forest, the chimpanzee has his rival's
cracked skull in his hands and laps the brains out.

A military officer sets fire to a Koran,
and starts a flame bigger than he imagined.

Rockets pop off making arcs like shooting
stars and a father tells his children to make a wish.


## The Mat
        by Gabe Shulman

soaked and sopping
from a storm last night,
instead of drying the feet,
    wets them.

Walking down the hallway—
I turn to witness the glossy prints
on the wooden surface.
Evidence that I was ever there
    in the first place.


## A Poem from my Bedroom Window
        by Gabe Shulman

If I were to write a poem now,
it would probably be about the boat
across the street in the vacant lot,
forever shored and lonely,

or the donkey who grazes there,
moping around the boat at dusk,


or the pseudo-vaquero
who pulls up in a red Mustang,
to ride the donkey instead,

or the old woman
with the black umbrella,
and her navy dress,
walking the afternoon sun,

slipping by like a silhouette
of the wicked witch,

or the kid in headphones,
playing basketball by himself
until the dawn fades
and it all begins again,
begins again.


## Shoulders
by Gabe Shulman

Would that Da Vinci had put down his plume
and gone to work the wheat fields
for lack of a better reason,
or had Einstein let his mind overtake him
and wandered the streets in rags,
muttering to strangers
or had Newton been knocked out by the apple
and simply never woke up
from the coma,
we'd be Kubrick's ape men, knocking
with our alabaster bones, breaking them
upon the abysmal surface of the Monolith,
left wondering,
how to make that great black door sway.


## W.
by Gabe Shulman

He sits down in a lawn chair
waiting for the sun to fall behind the
cedar, dry mesquite and old oaks,
bringing the veil of night
like a fly net over everything.
In the humid air, a cold cervesa sweats
alongside a lukewarm bottle of J.D.
resting down on the floorboards.

The evening redness grows in the west,
the sun falls heavy beyond the barren mesa
like an old orange dinner plate being closed
in the drawer until the next family dinner.

A single porch light glows where moths
and skeeters swarm like mad and the coons
and opossums start to sneak up from the edge
of the trees to snake the dog food laid out.

The dogs start to holler at the sight of them,
he calms them with a few angry yells
and goes back to his drinking.

He looks out and sees God in all things,
himself, his country, his war.
The mosquitoes nip
at the back of his sweaty neck, trying
to get his boozed blood.
He forgives them all,
even though they tried and tried
like dogs to tear him apart
limb from limb.
It took him years
to learn to forgive.

He looks at a painting he'd just finished
the night before, propped against the house
and wonders;
What is it that compelled him to paint
Putin's face so raw and majestically?
He wonders what it is that compels
a man to do anything,
but then remembers that it was God,
who sank the earth
when man became too greedy,
who toppled the tower of Babylon,
when man became too great.

He looks out into the balmy, swarming night
and thinks of all God had to do in his time,

how once even, that He was seen as a tyrant
when his righteous waves crashed upon the land
and concludes,
*Yeah I done good, I done good.*


## Baby Grand
###### by Trampas Smith

He thought he was the God damned belle of the ball,
and maybe he was: fortified to the gills he swaggered
till he staggered from the bourbon and the beer and
the bourbon. Now he leans against a backyard fence
confiding in the horse the host had boasted of placing in the Bellmont
    Stakes.
The steak! Tartar. Great God, had it been
delicious? A sweet slimy slab he had devoured,
terminating the talk with some broker of mergers,
and now that cow flesh festers and grows in his gut,
like the ghoul in that movie that erupts from a stomach
and dashes, crashing through dishes, ruining dinner. . . .
Sure as sunrise, it *is* coming out, but in the usual way.
Feet apart, fingernails take the rail like angry teeth and
retch goes the wretch. Retch, wretch, retch.
And after, trembling electric, all is new again.
The moon stares down, glorious and bored.

The horse whinnies and stamps: offended.
Snobs are everywhere.

Inside, silhouettes mingle. The piano plays,
its faint familiar tune like a scent on the breeze:
tepid decoration for so many monologues.
No, none listens but to themselves, and scarcely that.
And none misses me, thinks he. But I know that song.
Yes, he knows the chords, and those of a few more.
Crowdpleasers, showstoppers even. Ragtime reborn.
Indeed, with a fresh clean face and a whiskey
watered down, show them what they've been missing.
Take the bench and bang those horse teeth, baby,

make them sing, unify, rise and shine.
The night is yet young, and it's all within reach,
with a highball on a napkin, atop the baby grand.


## Saw a Wild Thing
### by Trampas Smith

In a rusting backyard chair he sits, surrounded:
the gray fence failing, the once garden overrun,
shovel blade bitten by the earth and her gloves
dry and shrunken atop the shaft. He gave up
bacon, beer and cigarettes, so he only sits,
awaiting instructions: she tells him things.
Birds in the new-green trees only sing.
The weather is so perfect, it is like
nothing at all.

Then a *POOF* on the ground before him,
pluming dust, a wad of leaves and sticks:
some rare phlegm coughed up by the earth?
No, it is moving, and he is up, knees cracking dry,
heart swelling, wind strangling, shuffling forth he finds
squirrels.

Slightly bigger than babies and dazed are
three furry rodents unfocused and writhing,
their nest, failed cradle, unravelling around them.
He stoops, thinking bottles of milk, shelled pecans
a wire wheel, when a manic presence jolts him upright.
Snarling, chittering, bristling, quivering, deranged, this is
the mother.

He starts to grin but she lunges, a stabbing feint of tooth and claw,
correcting him, her eyes gone agoggle and white hot.
She needs space to figure and he gives it, backs away to his seat.
She darts about her brood, dives in and pulls one out
by skin of its neck and scurries with her little sack of squirrel toward
the tree.

On the trunk she pauses, gathering strength for her child is heavy,
sagging against her, but still without self pity she goes on up,
pausing again at the first fork, then out onto a branch.
At the next fork, in the sun, she releases it onto
the sky, where the nest was. He watches it
fall and go *THUMP* beside the others.
And she reappears, reassesses,
bites another.


## Catch-and-Release
by Molly Stewart

Somewhere between grass-stained jeans, and
Laying in the sun just to appreciate the breeze, and
Fishing trips, catch-and-release, and
Hide-and-go seek, you can't catch me, and
Summer-sweet, street light reminders, and
Simple rules, Keepers are Finders, and
Happy souls, carefree and full, and
The first friend who didn't come home, and
Getting a taste of life after this, and
Trying to hold it all as it slipped, and
Discovering first loves often don't last, and
Losing your self as you create your past, and
Finding yourself in the shade of the setting sun, and
Hiding in the shadow thrown by the things you should've done, and
You take what you need and pass on the rest, and
You find time to lay in the breeze, catch your breath, and
You recognize life isn't to keep, but catch-and release.


## My Heart Burns for the Love of That Girl
by Molly Stewart

Sweet-tarts of calcium,
You crunch in my teeth and,
Travel down my throat to,
Soothe the angry beast who,
Sleeps inside of me where,

My child grew from,
The size of a pea to,
A six-pound four-ounce
Heartburn-evoking
Baby who,
Turned me into
A mother who,
Has had heartburn
Every day for the
Last seven years and,
Now eats calcium sweet-tarts
Like every day is Halloween.


## Season's Shadows
### by Molly Stewart

Season's shadows
Collect like leaves in trees,
Fading over time,
To muted browns,
quietly falling away.
Traveler in memories,
How fog creates depths,
In steps along paths
with the who and if
Becoming ideas of past.


## Brilliance is Messy
### by Jackie Tuesday

The lightbulb
That contains my mind
Shatters,
Prohibiting me from find-
-ing any cohesive thought.

Ideas thrown
About in space,

Fractures
The porcelain face
I try to keep polished.

Brilliance is messy.
All inspiration
Scatters
Through my exaggeration,
Creating colorful cadences on canvas.

Let go, don't force
Your creativity to
Flatter
The world about you.
Your art is like masturbation.

Art, brilliance, genius,
All come from a chaos that
Patterns
Itself into solid fact
That can be used to understand.

I am thankful that my lightbulb shattered,
Fractured,
Fanned out when it scattered.
It flatters in patterns, my broken soul.


## Defective
by Jackie Tuesday

Broken, not machine but man
Machines can restart
Humankind can only die.

# Reflective Transparency
by Jackie Tuesday

I hold a stone like glass
From an old church window.
Hues of blue and purple blend
With transparency, clouded clarity.

There are visible signs of brokenness inside,
But it is barely felt on the surface.
It looks so light, but is heavy.
Its beauty and cracks seem to weigh it down.

I understand that weight,
The assumed transparency,
The broken bits that change the way the light is reflected.
It is hard to be beautiful.

Your flaws shimmer like ocean waves breaking the shore.
They reflect the best in you.
I drown in your ocean,
In hopes you will reflect the best in me.


# Scholarly Pleasure
by Jackie Tuesday

Rows of endless knowledge
Sparkle in florescent lights.
Silence, complete and full
Fills my ears and heart.
The smell of seduction
Enters me through the musty pages.
The sweetest whispers of love and lust
I hear in the shuffling of the pages.
Rene Descartes, his meditations
My foreplay.
I cannot stop myself, my hand slips
Inside, touching paradise.
Considering Calderon's implications

Of life and dreams and oh!
Literature my provocative muse,
She woes me into euphoria.


## To Die in Battle
by Jackie Tuesday

I haven't been in the trenches
Of this world's unholy wars,
But I do create blockades, trenches
Of my own—I try to seal the doors

To my vulnerabilities, so to keep
My sanity. I am in the thick
Of battle, fighting—blind—in the deep
Of my subconscious. I have to pick

My defenses carefully, so to hide
My desperation. Internalize,
Put frustration aside,
Release myself from emotional ties,

Keep breathing, keep trudging,
March in step with fate,
Push through, in the tar sludging,
Crying, channel the hate.

That results from self-contempt.
Seize fire!
In war there is no fact
Or fiction, only mindless desire

From glory or peace or destruction.
With myself I sign a treaty, needing
The pain to end, but I already see the treason
Between me and myself. The bleeding

Caused by the mustard gas
Fills my lungs. I choke

On memories, regrets, holding fast
Until the last murderous stroke.


## In Your Shoes
by Mairi Vannella

My dear pupil,
My peer in the classroom,
And the stranger in the bus,
I wish you the best.

Your exterior shell,
Blemished, yet united,
Lends the world an impression
Of your tastes, dreams, and desires.

No one stranger truly knows
Your history, your struggles,
Your choices that provide the basis
For the image the world ultimately sees.

It is these same struggles,
Which haven't destroyed you,
That make you durable and wise—
And what truly makes you beautiful.


## The Lost Prayer
by Mairi Vannella

Teach me the skills to navigate this
Storm we call reality.
And, when I will likely shift,
Give me the courage and the kindness
To begin once more with hope,
Even though this too may be
Lost to the senses of silence.
Here, ceaselessly,
I plea for your mercy

And your undying, merciful love.
My heart speaks aloud of this—
Longing to spring forth anew,
From the ashes of a dim life,
As a new being.


## Mask
  by Mairi Vannella

The spirit awakens with heaviness,
Traversing its landscape
With the same bored intensity
That it carries during the seasons.
*She's perfectly content...*

Laughter and merriment fill the scenery,
And all is well in the space of time.
Euphoria takes his leave,
And rising tension hits the young spirit
As she finishes her lesson.
She ignores it, finds a mask,
And entertains her pupils.
*It's showtime.*

Her guide and a stranger
Find her hideout at last.
The shadows that stalk her
Ruthlessly, shamelessly,
Threaten to expose her façade
Called composure and mellowness.
Some concealer and masquera help out,

And she greets friends with open arms.
*The laughter is loud.*

Several beatings and miscommunications
Bring this entity to her knees.
She opens herself up
So that now her mentors, friends,

Loved ones, and herself
Can openly express mockery and disgust
Out of pride and self-loathing.
Seeing her faults, they toss water
Out of need for cleansing,
For she isn't completely melting.
*"Slay the beast."*

The spirit seeks solace in the shadows.
The mask comes off,
And she is naked in the eyes of night.
The salty pain slowly takes its toll,
For she collapses into a wrecked state
Like a hunted animal.
The water scalding her bones,
She welcomes the dark fog of fatigue
And defeat, finding a home
In its cold embrace.
... And she finds her release.


# Autumn Rhapsody
### by Quang Vo

I.
Love stories littered
the stream banks—
and if we could have plunged
our entropic forms into the
sunlit stream together,
would it have betrayed
or muddied the paleness
of our bodies? I dreamt
my veins became tree-roots
on the stream's edge, and
to dull rocks I gave that
firefly moment imagined
under water.

II.
Our car stopped on a road
beneath tall and heavy
trees aromatically full.
A whole day spent plucking
persimmons in the hilly
reaches of your arms.
I leaned, wept in your hair
and dosed over ripen
somnolent boughs.
I have no need of ladders—
only the boundlessness
of you under persimmon trees.

III.
The road home—
a silent Wagnerian scene:
so much to tell you,
yet there is no time.
You are somewhere
that does not bare
your blasé smile,
between the duct taped sky
you left picked blossoms
        by the stream.
What fallen nature sprout
itself in you and I
to packed time past
behind those autumn eyes?


# Jackfruit
        by Quang Vo

*To J.*

You pack some jackfruit
for lunch, forget to share your
intentions. I understand

the task is pensive,
messy, wonderful—
why share with me?

Your hands move patiently—
courting fingers fumbling
sunlit skin for resin pearls
nestling inside.

You savor each
bulb, torn as fibers
from the reed mat
under my childhood dreams.

And so,
my fingers are left idle, starving
while the seeds you remove
sparkle like polished stones.


# Thursday
by Quang Vo

*To J.*

Bubbles on cobbled steps—
like a field of glazed flowers.

I think of you, waiting under
a pigeon feathered sky

like a drenched kitten
with sadness harpstrung to her eyes—

two amber butterflies stirring
a sunbeam shard.

And raindrops wash all shyness
from your sun dodged face,

and I ask the seasons
not to dye your hair,

to preserve the color
of the southern fields,

though I am sweetly dark as  a
honey gatherer and timid as a caterpillar.

Your steps grow light, your figure
vanishes in the murky streets.


## Yellow Crane Aubade
### by Quang Vo

"Em ởi như cánh h c vàng,
Ngàn mãm mây tr ng ng  ngàng còn trôi"
(You walk like a yellow crane,
while shy clouds drift for a thousand years)
—Nguy n Hi n

*To J.*

This is how you walk: with a freshet of
hair over your shoulders. Late August

and you haunt me like a yellow crane—
its wings riding a river of sunlight.


At a distance, my sentiments settle on the
riverbed, tangled to the fate of silkworms.

Twenty is a beautiful age, your mother's
cherished year back to comfort her.

Your brother's ambitions turned
into stratus clouds where a flock of cranes

carried your father. *Can you see your daughter?*
He responds, coldly—with absence.


## Drunken Stupor
####     by Brady Walker

Soft lips and Roman fingertips,
I did not know you then.
Had I set sail upon that ship,
a man I could have been!

I feed these kids and plow this field,
yet if I was young again,
I'd drink and brawl and fight them all
with that same ol' devil's grin.

Instead I'm stuck on this old plot
with a wife who's fat as sin,
and not on that bright shining ship
where horizons never end!

If I could find that younger lad,
I'd say, "Don't ever settle in!
Board that ship and you'll become
the man I wish I could have been!"


## Ghazal Ghazal Ghazal
####     by Brady Walker

My professor told me to write a ghazal
but he knows no one likes the ghazal.

Redundant repetition abounds within
the confines of the immutable ghazal.

They tell me that I will see beauty inside
a Persian classic known as the ghazal.

Yet all I see is distasteful structure
combatting intuitive style within the ghazal.

The poem, in fact, can stretch on forever,
ad infinitum, et cetera, ghazal.


# Socially acceptable medium for violence
### by Brady Walker

Hunter and prey both fight and flight
While roles reverse in heated fray
The risk of bodily harm excites
Akin to savage, ancient days
The cries of war and strength ignite
My brothers push along beside
With every passing second I
taste iron and salt
as my heart pounds faster
my fingers twitch
in primal state
feed on weakness
thrive on rage
Crouch.
Touch.
Pause.
Engage!


# A Storm above Babylon
### by Brady Walker

I am the merciless, right hand of God
Before me stands my fallen brother
My sword hangs ready, flat and broad
Defiant stance, his face uncovered

Before me stands my fallen brother
Somewhere between dusk and dawn

Defiant stance, his face uncovered
The prince of Persia's sword is drawn

Somewhere between dusk and dawn
High above Babylon, death and ruins
The prince of Persia's sword is drawn
Prepared for battle, I call the legions

High above Babylon, death and ruins
With sacred decree I blow my horn
Prepared for battle, I call the legions
Fear the wrath of the Almighty Lord

With sacred decree I blow my horn
My sword hangs ready, flat and broad
Fear the wrath of the Almighty Lord
For I am the merciless, right hand of God

Manuel Ortiz Guerrero, 1897-1933

# School Affiliation of Contributing Writers

Onnyx Bei – University of St. Thomas
Travis Bowles – St. Mary's University
Alaina Bray – Lamar University
Erika Jo Brown – University of Houston
Keely Disman – Sam Houston State University
Jason Duncan – Texas State University
Theresa Ener – Lamar University
Donna Finney – Sam Houston State University
Casey Ford – Lamar University
Emryse Geye – Tarleton State University
James Johnson – Tarrant County College
Mercedes Kelso – St. Mary's University
Jennifer McFarland – University of Houston
Charles McGregor – University of Texas—Pan American
Grace Megnet – Lamar University
Matthew Mendez – St. Mary's University
Bryan Owens – University of Houston
Adrian Patenaude – Abilene Christian University
Brandy Rains – Abilene Christian University
MacKenzie Regier – Texas Tech University
Sammantha Rodriguez – St. Mary's University
Erica Saucedo – Tarleton State University
Ashton Secundino – Angelo State University
Genesis Senteno – University of Texas—Pan American
Huma Sheikh – Texas A&M University
Gabe Shulman – Texas State University
Trampas Smith – Texas Tech University
Molly Stewart – Tarleton State University
Jackie Tuesday – St. Mary's University
Mairi Vannella – St. Mary's University
Quang Vo – University of St. Thomas
Brady Walker – Tarleton State University